A SEAT AT THE TABLE

A SEAT AT THE TABLE

WOMEN, DIPLOMACY, AND LESSONS FOR THE WORLD

Irene & Mark,
Thank you for
your support on this
book and friendship
over the years.

SUSAN SLOAN

NEW DEGREE PRESS

A SEAT AT THE TABLE

Women, Diplomacy, and Lessons for the World

ISBN   978-1-64137-577-1 *Paperback*

        978-1-64137-578-8 *Kindle Ebook*

        978-1-64137-579-5 *Ebook*

DEDICATION

———

To my paternal grandmother, Bubbie, the diplomat of
our family who welcomed all with grace and dignity.

To my mother, Momma Sloan, who continues to
teach me the value of work and independence.

To my niece, Sloan, who will hopefully see gender
equality and diversity around the table.

CONTENTS

PROLOGUE

———

The cool air dissipated into the warmth of the new spring season. I stepped out on New Hampshire Avenue for a gala and entered the grand Whittemore House through a sea of black ties and floor-length gowns. This Washington, D.C. mansion is also known historically as the Women's National Democratic Club. The club originated in 1922, shortly after the passage of the 19th Amendment granting American women the right to vote. This famous location boasts prominent women members and was the venue for historical radio broadcasts from Eleanor Roosevelt. In this house steeped in rich female history, I joined the elite crowd for a reception and seated dinner. Having attended my fair share of receptions and galas, what struck me about this particular event was that the organization honored five women leaders: two ambassadors, a Major General, a U.S. Marine Corps Captain, and a top philanthropic plastic surgeon. The president of the organization hosting the gala was also a woman.

In all honesty, rarely do I hear moving speeches at galas and receptions. We network, eat, drink, and quietly whisper during the keynote remarks. But that evening, you could hear a pin drop. The honorees shared their moving stories, and the tears rolled down my cheek onto my silk jacket. These thoughts crossed my mind—who is capturing these stories? Who is sharing the impact of gender-diversified leadership?

* * *

I must confess: I am not a diplomat or a "foreign service officer." This book was inspired by my frequent interactions with American and foreign diplomats in my position at a nonprofit advocacy organization. I visit embassies for private events where the appetizers flow endlessly, and the open bar attracts the Washington social scene. Of course, the main attraction is typically the ambassador and a member of the U.S. presidential administration.

In Washington, I have found foreign service officers and members of Congress to be *our* celebrities. While the paparazzi may not swarm the streets following our cars, we typically do know the sound of certain motorcades bustling down Pennsylvania and Massachusetts Avenues. Diplomats have always intrigued me. Through my professional network, personal connections, and living in Washington, I've been able to enter their worlds and hear about their travels and experiences of major historical moments.

In private conversations—whether held over the phone while I sat at my kitchen counter, or face-to-face in elegant historic embassies or classic Washington offices—I asked the same questions of these leaders. In these conversations, most replied, "No one has ever asked me that."

In this book, I aim to cover the influence of women in as many regions of the world as possible. The included interviews touch on different themes, and I hope the lessons resonate with you as they did with me.

Along the way, the women diplomats and dignitaries I interviewed revealed intimate details of the quest for diplomacy, their experiences, and the tremendous impact of their work. Their work has saved lives around the world, led to treaties and peace processes, and strengthened alignment in many countries. More than that, these stories have opened a treasure trove of secrets illuminating how to balance family life with an ever-changing career. This is an aspiration of both men and women of the upcoming generation. In fact, one study found that young Millennials and Gen Z chose "work-life balance" as the most important aspect of a career, ranking it above advancement, organization mission, culture, and healthcare or benefits.[1]

One particular interview illustrated how much women have advanced in the foreign service and, more broadly, the passion required to pursue any goal. Barbara Bodine never imagined her "dysfunctional" upbringing in the San Fernando Valley would lead to her positions as a U.S. Ambassador to Yemen and Deputy Chief of Mission in Kuwait. Bodine heard the word "no" frequently throughout her childhood. Rather than becoming dissuaded, she understood that an education and career were her ticket out. In high school, she discovered her passion

---

1   "Study: Comparing Compensation & Culture of Millennials & Gen Z." Comparably, accessed September 8, 2019.

for diplomacy and desire to see the world and work on important issues.

Bodine recounts the gender dynamics of pursuing "law, medicine, or . . . a Ph.D.," or any profession besides an elementary school teacher, nurse, or secretary. As a woman, she was going to change the dynamics the minute she got into the room and sat at the table. The question was whether she could get into the room at all—only then could she ultimately find a seat at the table. "That was the overwhelming environment," she reflects. What she didn't know during high school was that this discovery would set off a dramatic chain of events, leading her to live in multiple countries and even becoming an ambassador.

When Bodine looks back at the progress of women in the foreign service, she sees that it has moved quite fast. Bodine was posted to the U.S. State Department's Bureau of East Asia Affairs in the '70s, then recruited to the Near East Bureau, and was one of the first women to get Chinese and Arabic language training. Her work in the Office of Arabian Peninsula Affairs—including security assistance for all the Arab Gulf States and her work as Country Officer for Yemen—defined the rest of her career. Twenty years later, when she was posted as the U.S. Ambassador to Yemen, her Deputy Chief of Mission, political officer, economic officer, and the head of her consular section were all women with Arabic language training. During Bodine's time in the foreign service, she saw the progress of women—once stymied by the lack of language training—grow to comprise an entire embassy of language-qualified, high-level officers. "Now that is a tremendous change," notes Bodine. Her story is continued in Chapter 1 and 13.

I wanted to see whether Bodine's story was unique or if it represented a powerful shift toward more women around the table. In 1970, women constituted less than 5 percent of foreign service officers and only 1 percent of senior-level officers. By 2003, women represented one-third of the officer corps and 25 percent of senior levels.[2] To put that in perspective, the 2019 Fortune 500 list of highest-grossing firms has thirty-three women CEOs on it—in other words, women only represented 6.6 percent.[3] Yes, both sectors saw progress, but not parity.

While gender diversity has changed in the foreign service, the personal stories of challenges and triumphs of women in this field are seldom heard. To share that knowledge, women must have a seat at the table. In Washington, foreign policy panels afford leaders the opportunity to share these experiences, but records show that in 2018 only one woman presented for every three men.[4]

While the life of a woman diplomat may not seem different than that of a man, my interviews demonstrate that their perspective is largely underreported. Though women leaders are showcased on television, radio interviews, newspapers, and magazines, they rarely share the intimate details of their experience or the stories behind the challenges they faced. On Washington's many foreign policy panels, the presence

2   Leon Weintraub, "Five Myths About the Foreign Service," *The Washington Post,* July 20, 2017.

3   Claire Zillman, "The Fortune 500 Has More Female CEOs Than Ever Before," *Fortune,* May 16, 2019.

4   Federiga Bindi and Mimosa Giamanco, "Missing in Action: The Absence of Women Scholars on Foreign Policy Panels," *Georgetown Journal of International Affairs,* March 26, 2019.

of women or lack thereof pierces the air like a blow-horn. "Since 2014, the presence of women on foreign policy panels in Washington, D.C. has grown by nine percent, increasing from 25 percent to 34 percent. With this level of growth, gender parity on foreign policy panels in D.C. will be achieved by 2025."[5] Fingers crossed; it will take both men and women to make it happen.

Although the presence of women in the foreign service is increasing, the gender gap in diplomacy and decision making persists. In a 2018 Canadian article discussing gender balance in the foreign service, the Pew Research Center reported that women made up only 36 percent of American ambassadors and 19 percent of U.K ambassadors in 2016.[6] Greater gender diversity in the diplomatic sector, as well as others, will lead to more diversified perspectives of the world's most pressing challenges and, ultimately, more thoughtful outcomes.

As a colleague of mine mentioned to me, the importance of gender diversity can be traced back to primal gender strengths. Men were traditionally hunters with singular focus, and women were gatherers, seeing the entire environment around them. Former Uber Chief Brand Officer Bozoma Saint John expands on this, "I think that women have a unique talent of being able to see the forest and the trees at the same time. We're able to sort of see the bigger picture and see the vision, but also see the unique things that

---

5   Ibid.
6   Catherine Tsalikis, "The Making of a Gender-Balanced Foreign Service: Stories from the Women Driving Canada's Diplomatic Corps Toward Equality," *OpenCanada*, April 3, 2018.

are happening and be able to fix [them]." The combination of focus and widespread vision is powerful.

This perspective may also be why women diplomats often have unique access to the inner workings of a country's culture, particularly if socially conservative. It has been noted that "female security sector officials frequently have access to populations and venues that are closed to men, which allows them to gather intelligence about potential security risks."[7] These foreign service officers can connect with women civilians on the ground in ways that men officers cannot. "When officers meet with women, they can provide fuller reports of the political, economic, and security situation. They can ask about the welfare of the children, whether they attend school and if they can safely walk to school."[8] Considering social and political implications through the lens of their impact on families enables women diplomats to gain valuable insight about a country's complex situation.

My research on gender diversity demonstrates the same conclusion in other governmental sectors: "The participation of civil society groups, including women's organizations, makes a peace agreement 64 percent less likely to fail."[9] Thoughtful leadership and peaceful resolutions are vital in navigating geopolitical climates and well-armed countries. Gender diversity is crucial.

7   "Women's Participation in Peace Processes," Council on Foreign Relations, updated January 30, 2019.

8   Andrea Strano, "Foreign Service Women Today: The Palmer Case and Beyond," *The Foreign Service Journal*, March 2016.

9   "Women's Participation in Peace Processes," Council on Foreign Relations, updated January 30, 2019.

A Seat at the Table: Women, Diplomacy, and Lessons for the World is not about pitting women against men, female superiority, or trite cheerleading for women empowerment. With many countries facing severe challenges of migration, terrorism, climate change, and the spread of fast-paced technology, the people around the table will change the course of history and how leaders solve critical global problems.

The year 2020 marks the one hundredth anniversary of women's suffrage in the U.S. Throughout this century, women have utilized this freedom to speak and vote on many issues, including exercising agency over their salary, attaining equal representation in government, or securing the custody of children. Much like a home, a country is a complex set of systems and social norms. For centuries, women have led in different capacities, and in this generation, diverse voices in leadership are making waves and inciting social change. In the foreign service sector, we hope that the increase in diverse voices will lead the world to a brighter, more diplomatic future.

A note to male readers: these lessons are just as much for you as they are for women. A handful of men allies helped secure interviews. They were supportive of the topic and aided in getting momentum. Men allies are just as important in the struggle for gender parity, and gender parity positively impacts everyone.

These pages tell the stories of women leaders playing a fundamental part in combatting ISIS, negotiating treaties, setting standards for cybersecurity, and handling intense conflicts—all while balancing family responsibilities with working abroad and enduring a double standard to rise in the ranks.

This book is written for:
- Aspiring women leaders
- Men allies who want to champion gender equality
- Future generations who aim to create better solutions for our countries

These collected stories contain candid advice on how to succeed not only in the diplomatic sphere, but also in life. They demonstrate how not to take up the shield and sword but instead to use dialogue and teamwork for solutions—a lesson for all sectors. Any gender can benefit from this knowledge. Understanding and leveraging the power of diverse voices will foster the next era of diplomacy and peace. The women featured here exemplify how an education and career allow individuals to reach the ultimate goal of being an authentic leader with a seat at the table.

PART 1

DIPLOMACY: THE SHORT AND LONG OF IT

CHAPTER 1

BEING FIRST

———

"I think the truth of the matter is, people who end up as 'first' don't actually set out to be first. They set out to do something they love, and it just so happens that they are the first to do it."

—CONDOLEEZZA RICE
FIRST AFRICAN AMERICAN WOMAN
U.S. SECRETARY OF STATE

Though many people strive to be the best in their field, being first isn't easy. With no predecessors, there is no precedent and little guidance. It can seem there's nothing to reach for nor a goal post to surpass. However, this also presents the freedom for trailblazers to create their own destinies.

In reflecting back on the history of diplomacy, I asked myself: when was the first time I learned about it? My mind traveled to Egypt and the biblical story of Moses. Moses approaches the pharaoh in a diplomatic mission of sorts, asking for his people to be set free. There is no declaration of war—just the simple "ask." As is depicted in the timeless and epic film *The Ten Commandments*, Moses simply says, "Let my people go." It is a simple ask, albeit a big ask. This was a diplomatic request, but where are the women in this mission?

In retrospect, maybe the entire diplomatic mission was actually set in motion by women. The mother of Moses cast her son into the Nile, and pharaoh's daughter rescued Moses and raised him as her own. Without the bravery and confidence of those women, who knows what might have happened?

While gender parity in the foreign service is on the rise, acknowledging how we got here will help us continue to progress. There are roadblocks to being first, but courageous women have and will bulldoze through them. As the former U.S. Ambassador to Yemen Barbara Bodine says, hearing "no" all the time can free you, because you have no other option but to turn it into "yes."

Bodine graduated Phi Beta Kappa and magna cum laude from the University of California, Santa Barbara, in 1970 with a concentration in Political Science and East Asian Studies. She earned her master's degree at the Fletcher School of Law and Diplomacy at Tufts University, where she was one of nine women in the program. Bodine's straightforward approach means business. Her take-no-prisoners attitude comes from inner self-reliance. She entered the foreign service with assignments in the U.S. State Department's Bureau of East Asia and eventually became one of the first woman political-military officers.

Around 1974, while in her mid-twenties, Bodine received a diplomatic posting in Bangkok, Thailand. It was her second tour and she was one of nine political-military officers, but she was the only woman in the role. The group served under the third-ranking person in the Embassy—the Political-Military Counselor. Although the U.S. Embassy in Bangkok was one of the largest U.S. embassies, Bodine knew she had no status, no power, and no influence as a junior officer. This was apparent when her boss, the Counselor, told the Ambassador and Deputy Chief of Mission, "I'm not sure about the women in the foreign service thing, and I'm not sure about this woman political-military officer thing. There is no way in G-d's Earth I am having a woman in my political-military section." Fortunately, the Ambassador and the Deputy Chief of Mission were not swayed, and the Counselor was strong-armed into having a woman officer in his section, whether he liked it or not.

After arriving in Bangkok, the Counselor walked Bodine into her "office." She slowly looked around the small windowless room and saw a coffee pot, one hot plate, and a small refrigerator. "He literally put me in the office kitchen. It lacked a certain subtlety," she said with a tinge of humor. Bodine is memorable in this way—she speaks with a fiery precision while also being down-to-earth.

She quickly realized her boss was not going to give her anything to do. With no portfolio and no responsibilities, she read and learned about everything going on in the office. Bodine's fellow officers would support her by bringing her to meetings. She then reported the situation to the Head of Management for the Embassy. Bodine asked if she could be transferred to another political section or another consulate in Thailand so she could grow her portfolio and pursue State Department tenure.

Within a few months of her posting, along the famous scenic Chao Phraya River, Bodine was invited to a diplomatic dinner party on a small wooden boat with the Embassy Chief of Staff, the Ambassador, and the Deputy Chief of Mission. The Ambassador asked Bodine how the posting was going. She responded blandly without mentioning her lack of duties, not wanting to rock the (literal) boat. The Chief of Staff looked at her and said, "Barbara, tell the Ambassador what's happening." Remaining as measured and composed as possible, Bodine explained the situation. The Ambassador and Deputy Chief of Mission listened politely but did not respond. Nothing further on the topic was said, and the group enjoyed the rest of the dinner along the river.

A couple weeks later, Bodine ran into the Ambassador in the hallway. He quietly asked her, "Oh, Miss Bodine, can you hold on for another couple of weeks?" She was sure she was going to be transferred. Surprisingly, the Counselor was sent back to Washington to retire. Bodine's response was "holy tadpoles!" The new Political-Military Counselor included her in the work and made her his unofficial Chief of Staff in addition to ensuring her tenure and promotion. This change allowed Bodine to work on assignments and advance her negotiation skills. That's when she realized it was possible—she could excel in the foreign service. Allies had supported her and wanted her to succeed.

Unfortunately, this wasn't the case for all women, especially in the 1970s. Many U.S. career diplomats from that era recall the famous Palmer Case. Alison Palmer originally joined the U.S. State Department in 1955. In 1968, she filed the first equal employment opportunity complaint in the foreign service. Bodine reflects that she did not sign on to the complaint, as she felt the majority of her colleagues aimed to help her succeed. Palmer won the complaint and then took on another class-action lawsuit challenging discriminatory criteria for women in the foreign service, inspired by the 1964 Civil Rights Act. The American Foreign Service Association states, "Today's impartial entrance criteria, evaluation and promotion policies, and assignments processes all stem in large part from 'the Palmer Case,' which was fought in various phases over more than 30 years."[10]

In our conversation, Bodine notes that before the Palmer Case, men allies had increased opportunities for women by hiring them for non-conventional jobs and bureaus. The *status quo* was shifting, and there were men allies stepping forward to encourage young women officers in spite of systemic resistance.

Bodine claims the U.S. Foreign Service shifted when the State Department reversed a rule banning women diplomats from getting married, but she qualifies that it was much more than that. Technically, in the 1970s, the marriage law had evolved and allowed women to marry someone who was retired or from another profession. However, women still couldn't marry another active duty foreign service officer. The rule didn't bother Bodine as much as the "truly insidious restriction" that women officers couldn't get advanced language training or get a "hardship post."

---

10 Andrea Strano, "Foreign Service Women Today: The Palmer Case and Beyond," *The Foreign Service Journal*, March 2016.

"If you can't learn Japanese, Chinese, Russian, Arabic, and a few of the other hard languages that are key for either allies or competitors, and you can't go to dangerous or difficult posts, you restrict women officers to Western Europe and a few places in Latin America," remembers Bodine. It was a road with no end. If women couldn't learn Arabic, they weren't going to be posted to the Middle East. If women couldn't learn Chinese or other Asian languages, they would be excluded from diplomatic postings in Beijing, Hong Kong, Tokyo, and Singapore. For Bodine, the change of the language training rule "really blew the foreign service open for women," allowing them to work anywhere in the world.

Along with many other interviewees, Bodine identifies the awareness of gender dynamics as the central difference between men and women. She says men don't tend to notice when other women aren't in the room. "Guys generally are kind of clueless about the treatment of women and women's opportunities. I mean, even if they're not hostile or aggressively trying to block [progress], they are just clueless. They just don't see it. They do not notice if there are no women in the room, whereas a woman would notice immediately."

The same statement is made about minorities—noticing inequities is half the battle. To be an ally of women or marginalized voices, we must look around the table. How many women are present? Are there people of color? Are more than three religious groups represented? Gender parity and diversity will only progress when everyone notices the absence of certain groups around the table.

Bodine also shares this story with her students at the Georgetown University School of Foreign Service. "I think I use this story to [demonstrate] how to handle a problem. You don't have to accept the situation, but you must handle it [wisely]." Using internal wisdom to determine when to speak up and when to stay silent is a balancing act. She mentions the value of finding allies and supporters to help make a reasonable request. To own your career, you must take responsibility. Bodine says, "You don't have to passively accept" something that isn't working. When she thinks back to her time in Bangkok, she realizes that she couldn't assume everybody knew what was happening. Being responsible for oneself by setting a solution in motion is important. If you can't solve an issue by yourself, the first step is letting other people know and finding allies who can help you solve it.

With more than thirty years in the foreign service, Bodine's story is one of many. From 1980 to 1983, Bodine served as the deputy principal officer at the U.S. Embassy in Baghdad. Later in 1990 to 1991, she served as the number two in Kuwait as the Deputy Chief of Mission during the Iraqi invasion and occupation. She is the recipient of the U.S. Secretary of State's Award for Valor for her work in occupied Kuwait. Part 4 of this book will dive deeper into Bodine's work in Kuwait and how it saved lives and protected many vulnerable people.

While digging through articles and exploring when women started making their mark in diplomacy, I found similar roadblocks to what Bodine faced. For example, after "40 years of the establishment of Canada's external affairs department in 1909, only men were allowed to write the foreign service entrance examination—if a woman wanted a career in diplomatic work, she had to settle for a job as a secretary or a clerk." [11]It wasn't until 1947 that Canadian women were permitted to take the foreign service examination and become officers. Both Canada and the U.S. had similar rules that forced women to choose between marriage or a diplomatic career. In the U.S., few women became diplomats prior to the 1970s due to the requirement that women officers resign when they got married. This institutionalized policy finally changed, which cracked the glass ceiling barring more women from entering foreign policy. In Canada, the shift of gender equality in diplomatic representation is occurring as I write this book. In 2013, around 29 percent of Canada's top diplomats were women, with an increase in 2017 to 44 percent. [12]

In 2015, Hungary saw its first woman Ambassador to Washington, D.C.; her experience is discussed in depth later in the book. The following year, King Mohammed VI from the Kingdom of Morocco swore in Princess Lalla Joumala Alaoui as the first woman Moroccan Ambassador to the U.S. I had the pleasure of meeting her briefly when she first came to Washington for a work event. Alaoui was gracious, elegant, and well-spoken; Morocco had truly sent one of its finest diplomats to the city. The year 2019 saw the appointment of Princess Reema bint Bandar from Saudi Arabia become its first woman Ambassador to Washington. In

---

11   Catherine Tsalikis, "The Making of a Gender-Balanced Foreign Service: Stories from the Women Driving Canada's Diplomatic Corps Toward Equality," *OpenCanada*, April 3, 2018.

12   Ibid.

Moscow, Wing Commander Anjali Singh became India's first woman military diplomat in 2019. [13]

Why is the Washington, D.C. post so important? From my interviews and research, I discovered that women foreign service officers were historically placed in "light" postings—places with less influence and discord, or as the U.S. State Department calls it, the opposite of "hardship" postings. While Washington is far from a hardship posting, as it's not in a war-torn nation or high-risk region, it's considered the center of the power vortex. Foreign ministries send their best and brightest to the city to influence foreign policy.

Careers are made in Washington, along with decisions that reverberate throughout the entire world. If you're posted here early in your career as a diplomat, there's a high probability you'll excel to a higher position. Being posted in Washington as an ambassador or number two at an embassy—the Deputy Chief of Mission (DCM)—is a career milestone. The power or prestige of Washington postings is one thing, but the central role you play in building your country's foreign policy and security pursuits is far more important. Washington has the power to position people for a larger seat at a table.

While the number of women diplomats is increasing, a 2016 foreign policy analysis showed that women made up only 25 to 40 percent of the ambassadors representing their countries.

---

13   "Wing Commander Anjali Singh Becomes India's First Female Military Diplomat," Livemint, updated September 17, 2019.

[14]These countries led the way in women ambassador appointments, but we haven't yet reached gender parity:

- Finland: 44 percent
- The Philippines: 41 percent
- Sweden: 40 percent
- Norway: 33 percent
- The United States: 30 percent
- Canada: 29 percent
- Colombia: 28 percent

As of 2020, Sweden has increased its percentage of women ambassadors to 48 percent, according to the Ministry for Foreign Affairs in Sweden. Many of the women interviewed for this book were "firsts" at some point in their careers. Though this is often referred to as "breaking the glass ceiling," I think of it as getting a seat at the table. Not in the back of the room. Not outside in the hallway. And not in some cubicle in the catacombs of the basement. *At* the table—as leaders, decision-makers, and foreign policy experts.

I don't like thinking of these women as being tokenized to fill some indivisible quota, but rather as leaders in their own right who just happen to be women. As the Ambassador of Sweden to the U.S. Karin Olofsdotter points out in a very straightforward manner, she has never thought of herself as a woman in her role. She's always been a diplomat—plain and simple. Being a woman set her apart in a crowd with a Prime Minister but compared to "the gray hair and gray suits," that's an advantage. "We look different, we are different," she attests.

---

14 Ann Towns and Birgitta Niklasson, "Gender, International Status, and Ambassador Appointments," *Foreign Policy Analysis* 13, No. 3 (2016): 521-540.

Within the context of national economies, former Austrian Foreign Minister Ursula Plassnik says, "Neither the private nor the public sector can afford to disregard 50 percent of its talent, energy, and experience."

Some countries have gone further in adapting gender parity as a national priority. In 2014, the Swedish Government was the first to declare itself a feminist government with a feminist foreign policy. This was in response to the persistent discrimination and systematic subordination of countless women and girls around the world. Feminist foreign policy offers a vision for the future in which women and men are truly equal and free to live their lives as they choose. The focus of Sweden's Feminist Foreign Policy is to increase the three "Rs":

- **Rights:** promoting full human rights for women and countering any discrimination
- **Representation:** supporting women's participation and involvement throughout the hierarchies of decision-making in both the public and private sectors
- **Resources:** full access to economic resources for all genders

Countries and companies are seeing how both halves of their populations benefit from gender equality. The overwhelming message of my interviews and conversations is that women are well suited for diplomacy. The required skill sets of active and patient listening, empathy, compassion, strategy, and resilience are in a woman's toolbox. Learned behavior and instinct make women successful diplomats. (Plus, try doing all those things in heels. If that's not daily resilience, I don't know what is.) But in all seriousness, gender diversity brings forth better ideas and outcomes. Rather than seeing issues through a singular lens that doesn't accurately represent a population, the lens of gender parity enables greater clarity.

To be clear, both women and men are needed around the table. It's only together that we will be able to move forward. Throughout this book-writing process, I saw it in action. Men eagerly introduced me to their women colleagues, mentors, and friends for interviews. The sisterhood of women rose to the occasion, too. It was as if I had thrown a ball of twine into the air and women and men kept passing it around, introducing me to ambassadors, diplomats, and government officials. The twine created an intricate web that gave me hope and a sense of security that people were working together to weave and uphold the fabric of society. It's through their efforts that lives are saved, wars are thwarted, and countries can live in peaceful coexistence—the ultimate goal of international relations.

CHAPTER 2

THE HISTORY OF IT ALL

———

"Whatever title or office we may be privileged to hold, it is what we do that defines who we are ... each of us must decide what kind of person we want to be—what kind of legacy that we want to pass on."

—QUEEN RANIA AL ABDULLAH OF JORDAN

Giving a voice to women in the foreign service was initially slow-going. While women around the world have always been involved in monarchies and foreign relations, women participation as official diplomats was different. Women officially entered the U.S. foreign service around the 1920s, about 150 years after the country was founded, and they continued to cross barriers. Below are some of the historic trailblazers[15]:

———

15   "Women in the Foreign Service," Office of the Historian, Foreign Service Institute, United States Department of State, accessed · September 17, 2019.

- **1922: Lucile Atcherson** was one of the first women in the foreign service, passing the Diplomatic Service examination in 1922 with the third-highest score. On December 5, 1922, she was appointed Secretary in the Diplomatic Service. On April 11, 1925, she moved to Berne, Switzerland, on assignment as Third Secretary. In order to get married, Atcherson resigned on September 19, 1927.

- **1925: Pattie H. Field** was another first to enter the foreign service after the passage of the Rogers Act. Sworn in on April 20, 1925, Field served as a Vice Consul in Amsterdam. On June 27, 1929, she resigned as she accepted a position with the National Broadcasting Company.

- **1933: Congresswoman Ruth Bryan Owen Rohde** was the first American woman appointed to a high-level diplomatic post in 1933 as a minister to Denmark.[16]

- **1949: Eugenie Anderson** was appointed by President Truman as U.S. Ambassador to Denmark from 1949 to 1953. She served as the first woman appointed to the ambassador level in the U.S. foreign service. Through her work, she persuaded Denmark to strengthen its commitment to NATO. In 1950, she became the first American woman to sign a treaty, which she drafted—the Treaty of Commerce and Friendship with Denmark. At the end of her posting, King Frederik IX bestowed a high honor to Anderson with the Grand Cross of the Order of Dannebrog.

---

16   "Women Diplomats," The Library of Congress, American Memory, accessed September 17, 2019.

- **1965: Patricia Roberts Harris** was appointed on June 4, 1965, as Ambassador to Luxembourg. Historically, she was the first African American woman in U.S. history to hold the ambassador rank.

- **1972: Patricia "Patti" Morton** was the first woman to be appointed Diplomatic Security Special Agent.

- **1997: Madeleine Albright** famously served the United States as the first woman Secretary of State from 1997 to 2001.

With each decade, more women's voices come to the table and change history. While writing this book, I was graciously introduced to a woman who did just that. Most U.S. government officials recognize her name, as she was the first woman confirmed by the U.S. Senate as the Assistant Secretary of Defense. She has worked extremely close with the highest levels of military, U.S. Department of State, U.S. Department of Treasury, the CIA, and the NSA. Her background is impressive and fascinating regardless of gender identity.

The Honorable Mary Beth Long has piercing eyes and wears a suit typical of government employees or politicians. This accomplished woman is a foreign policy expert, business owner, and longtime, distinguished U.S. government official. Long has been featured in Forbes Magazine's Women Business Leaders list and received multiple awards from the United States Government. She is also recognized as a life member of the prestigious Council on Foreign Relations and International Institute for Strategic Studies.

After graduating magna cum laude from the Penn State University honors program in 1985 and earning a JD from Washington and Lee University School of Law, Long embarked on a winding journey. Starting in 1986, Long began her career at the Central Intelligence Agency (CIA) in the position of Operations Officer. Long was one of the first six women to be included in the CIA's Clandestine Operations in Dangerous Areas (CODA) advanced weapons course. One of her initial operations led her to Latin America, working undercover as a State Department official.

Her job at the U.S. Embassy was to work undercover as a foreign service officer and attend diplomatic functions. She attended bureaucratic meetings, elegant receptions, and diplomatic events while conducting covert operations, performing two jobs at once. Long encountered some rough situations early on in the field, including one with an indigenous, malicious terrorist group. Before her second assignment, she underwent the standard agency training and prep work. However, she still felt the CIA's expectations of her as a woman were low because she was entering an extremely militarized country with a strong machismo culture. They sent her with a few assignments but set a low bar, sending the message that she wouldn't be taken seriously as a woman. This sentiment did not stop Long from progressing forward.

While assigned to the Department of State, Long completed four to five assignments; in almost all postings, she was either the only woman or one of few engaging foreign interlocutors. There may have been one or two exceptions of women serving in consular sections. Long recalls one woman in the economic section during her assignment with the State

Department. "As far as the intelligence organization was concerned, with one exception, I was always the only woman," she remarks.

Within the intelligence field—which she considers part of the nation's broader foreign policy—Long recalls relatively few women assigned to actively engage on the intelligence front, let alone leadership positions. With few women to work with or look up to, it was challenging to see how her professional journey could grow. I was curious if the CIA had made any progress since Long's tenure. Had they made any strides in the advancement of women?

In 2013, an advisory group led by former Secretary of State Madeline Albright released the findings of a five-year CIA study on "Women in Leadership."[17] At that time, most government agencies believed the CIA to be a forerunner for gender equality: "Two of the CIA's directorates were led by women, the Executive Director of the Agency was a woman, and the first woman Deputy Director in the Agency's history, Avril Haines, had been appointed. Nearly half of the CIA's workforce was female."[18]

However, the report raised eyebrows because "despite high-profile appointments, many women at CIA were unable to break the glass ceiling. There were unconscious biases embedded in the culture of the Agency, as well as stumbling blocks that led to an unleveled playing field."[19] What the

---

17 "CIA Makes Progress on Women in Leadership," Central Intelligence Agency, July 11, 2018.
18 Ibid.
19 Ibid.

study does not elucidate is that very few women in those senior leadership positions worked in the operations field. In fact, according to Long, historically fewer than 10 percent of the senior positions in the operations field were held by women.

Secretary Albright made recommendations based on the report and, in June of 2013, an implementation team was formed to work on three core issues:

- Foster intentional development
- Value diverse paths
- Increase workplace flexibility

From these goals, the CIA established solutions to change the culture, thereby enabling more women to attain and thrive in leadership positions:

- Establish clear criteria for promotion to the Senior Intelligence Service (SIS)
- Require equity assurance training for officers who sit on promotion panels
- Improvements on how managers provide feedback to employees
- Launch a limited pilot program for telework in unclassified areas
- Strengthen awareness of flexible work options

As a result of these advancements, the year 2018 marked a demographic shift. Around 43 percent of CIA officers promoted to senior ranks were women. Furthermore, 36 percent of the Senior Intelligence Service (SIS) were women. And the CIA got its first woman Director, Gina Cheri Haspel. There's still a long way to go, but according to Long, it has "gotten better."

In spite of this, Long continues to question the real growth in Washington. From think tanks to conferences—regarding hard diplomacy issues such as security, treaties, weapons, and status of forces agreements—women's involvement is still the exception and "incredibly underrepresented in any kind of public dialogue."

The Carnegie Endowment for International Peace released an article stating that since 2014, the presence of women on foreign policy panels in Washington, D.C., has increased from 25 to 34 percent.[20] However, Long explained that maybe one or two women are chosen for a panel or serve as a moderator in order to hit an invisible women quota. However, women are overall "grossly underrepresented." The Carnegie Endowment for International Peace noted that in 2018 there was one woman for every three males on D.C. foreign policy panels with 27 percent of the panels being "manels," a term coined for men-only panels.[21]

Long is baffled by this. As she sees it, most women engage in diplomacy in many parts of their lives and society, particularly in well-developed, male-dominated professions such as diplomacy and foreign policy. Thus, it makes sense for women to be actively involved in this work.

---

20 Federiga Bindi and Mimosa Giamanco, "Missing in Action: The Absence of Women Scholars on Foreign Policy Panels," *Georgetown Journal of International Affairs*, March 26, 2019.

21 Ibid.

"It's a real shame because we do bring a different perspective," she comments. "We have skills that are innate," such as the ability to actively listen and successfully compromise. Long believes women develop these skills to simply exist in society, and these skills are notable assets in diplomacy. In Long's seventeen years of civil service in intelligence, diplomacy, and defense, she only once had a woman supervisor. Most of the time, she was the only woman working in a certain area.

Without women role models, leaders, or mentors to seek out, Long was alone in her journey. She relied on male colleagues as mentors to help shape her career. She felt male professionals had vast networks that women did not: "There are so few women who are senior, and they're so out of reach." Long's overarching challenge was to cultivate a top-down woman mentorship network within the government. Mentorship is important to Long—it's one of the reasons she was open to sharing her story with me.

She believes the government is working on that challenge, but it faces, in large part, a resource issue. "We don't have time to seek out other women who aren't readily available," says Long. It takes time to develop trust and find commonalities. She adds candidly, "You're busy, frankly, elbowing your way to the table." Women professionals have to be better prepared in the competitive environment, especially among male or foreign counterparts. She hates the term but described it as developing "sharp elbows" to get to the table.

To advance your career in the Department of Defense (DoD) as a woman in the highly male-dominated government agency is no small feat. From 2007 to 2009, Long served as the first woman civilian Assistant Secretary of Defense (ASD), which is DoD's equivalent of a four-star general in the military. In that position, she provided congressional testimony on multiple subjects, working directly with Secretaries of Defense Donald Rumsfeld and Robert Gates on high-level issues. She served as Chairperson to the High Level Group responsible for NATO's nuclear policy; the position reports directly to the Secretary General of NATO. Around the National Security Council table, she represented DoD on policy matters. Her leadership role focused on the International Security Affairs office in the Office of the Secretary of Defense, overseeing policy for the Middle East, Europe, and Africa.

During the interview, Long points out that during her time in the defense field, there weren't any equivalent high ranked women in the nearly 20,000-person-staffed Pentagon building. She remembers a woman deputy comptroller—the first woman in the position of overseeing the massive defense budget. Throughout her career, she has found male mentors and taught herself how to grow professionally.

Long recalls that one of her proudest moments serving in those roles was when Secretary Gates left a meeting and asked her to sit at the table to represent the United States. Long describes the table we've all seen on TV, with eighty people sitting around a series of flags and microphones. She listened intently, most likely with her glasses perched at the end of her nose as she is pictured in numerous photos. She even gave a vocal intervention—basically a comment—at one point.

During the meeting, Long received a note from someone behind her chair. She quickly and quietly grabbed it without turning around. She looked at the note and noticed it was in Secretary Gates' handwriting. He had snuck back into the meeting and was sitting directly behind her. Long remembers fondly that the note said, "Look around the room. You're the only woman." It was a powerful moment for her—she confesses she has that little yellow sticky note to this day.

It wasn't an easy ride becoming the first woman Assistant Secretary of Defense. In fact, Long says it was quite difficult and soul-crushing. As a woman, she faced numerous formal complaints during her confirmation that by law required vetting. The issues weren't substantive—rather, they focused on gender. How would the Arabs respect a woman? Shouldn't the position go to a former military officer? Did she sleep her way to the top of this male-dominated agency? Would her breast cancer come back and was it a threat? She wasn't married, so who was she dating? Long feels these questions were unbelievable. One might "expect that in the 1960s or 1970s," but not in contemporary society.

But Long wasn't going down without a fight. The FBI presented the choice of an internal or third-party investigation to review the formal complaints, proposing that the Inspector General conduct the investigation. She feared the "old boy network" would prevail on the issues. President Bush and the Secretary of Defense graciously told Long that it was up to her to either proceed anonymously or allow a third-party entity to objectively resolve the concerns. Long conceded and went with the full FBI investigation. "That's what I chose. It was miserable and the worst experience of my life," she confides.

The investigation affected her health and emotional well-being. She felt it was nothing short of devastating. She walked into work every day with the knowledge that her peers and subordinates all knew she was being investigated. Whether it was a side glance in a hallway or a feeling in a room, Long knew some of the people within the organization were working against her. She describes that some of the claims were simply "outrageous"—one allegation even claimed she traded sex for changes to the rules of military engagement. Despite all of this, Long acknowledges, "I suppose it was worth it."

After the investigation cleared her name and the confirmation happened, Long felt ecstatic, vindicated, and exhausted. She understood she would always have to watch her own back. She went home and cried for the better part of a weekend out of "sheer mortification, embarrassment, elation, [and] exhaustion."

While she is glad she was able to serve as Assistant Secretary of Defense, Long says in the same breath, "I'll never do the confirmation process again—never do it again, if that's what it takes."

Long says she didn't mind being scrutinized or jumping through the same hoops as men pursuing high-level appointments. However, almost 100 percent of the concerns were specific to her and gender-related, or in her own apt words, "sex allegation bullshit." It tainted her image for future appointments. In the Defense Department, Long was the first woman in such a role. The pursuit of her career and identity as a woman in that environment made advancement a mountainous, stressful climb.

At the end of our conversation, Long admits, "You're the first person I've talked about this with. I'm only just now starting to talk about what a disgrace the whole thing was. The nation should be ashamed that it was allowed to happen."

Long served as Assistant Secretary of Defense from 2007 to 2009. In 2009, she received high honors from the U.S. Government, including the award of the Secretary of Defense Medal for Outstanding Public Service, the DoD Medal for Distinguished Public Service, and the Chairman of the Joint Chiefs of Staff Distinguished Civilian Service Award. For those who don't know, the latter is the Pentagon's most prestigious civilian honor.

Long founded her first defense company, Metis Solutions, LLC, in 2010, which she then sold to a private equity firm around 2016. She is also the owner of MB Long & Associates, LLC law firm, which specializes in export compliance. On top of that, Long is the Founder and Principal at Global Alliance Advisors and owner of Askari Defense and Intelligence, LLC.

Having established her homegrown network, Long has been recognized for her unique skills sets by other power players. During Mitt Romney's 2012 presidential campaign, she was a senior advisor and a distinguished member of the campaign's intelligence transition team. During the 2016 presidential campaign cycle, she served as an expert commentator and was quoted on issues of foreign policy and national security.

Long stayed true to herself during the turbulent 2016 U.S. presidential election. According to the media, she was identified by Secretary of Defense James Mattis as his first choice for Undersecretary of Policy in the Office of the Secretary of Defense. While the position would have been an honor and a challenge, she did not receive the appointment after signing an open letter concerning President Trump's candidacy.[22]

It's not just the "firsts" that define the impact of women trailblazers, but also the motivation to keep pushing. Mary Beth Long and the women who came after her are creating deeper paths for gender parity in national security and diplomacy. The legacy of women in foreign policy will not be titles held or the scope of their obstacles, but rather their impact at the table—debating, adding, and pushing one another to create better solutions for the world.

---

22 David E. Sanger and Maggie Haberman, "A Letter From G.O.P. National Security Officials Opposing Donald Trump," *The New York Times*, August 8, 2016.

CHAPTER 3

STARTING FROM SCRATCH

———

"If you never encounter anything in your community that offends you, then you are not living in a free society."

—KIM CAMPBELL

FIRST WOMAN PRIME MINISTER OF CANADA

A nation's history of diplomacy starts before that country is formed. Select leaders travel to different nations to garner support for their people's independence. Sometimes this is military support, and other times it's financial aid. The pursuit of national independence takes the help of other nations. That is why diplomacy is imperative. Speaking with diplomats who have represented countries formed as recently as the 1990s has been a privilege. These nations' roads to independence and the struggles endured in forming a new system illustrate the fortitude required when starting from scratch.

Over chamomile ginger tea served on a silver tray, Ambassador Monica Nashandi opens our conversation: "I'll tell you the story of Namibia. It's a country that was colonized by the Germans for about thirty years, and then was under South African control for seventy years, including the apartheid time. Namibians launched a struggle for independence. In this struggle, women participated hand in hand with men."

Nashandi and I sit on black leather couches across from empty glass bookcases. A gold chandelier hangs over the long, shiny, wooden conference table. A single framed photo of the Namibian president rests atop the fireplace. All other framed photos have been taken off the walls as the Embassy is being renovated. Nashandi looks at me intently through her dark-rimmed rectangular glasses, demonstrating her concentration and openness. With short hair and a friendly demeanor, you would not guess that she once held a gun at the frontlines for Namibia's independence.

From the moment Nashandi begins, I know that the story about to unfold is going to give me chills. She paints a vivid picture of Namibian history, lamenting the exploitation, stolen resources, and discrimination of her people. "Women were doubly exploited," Nashandi argues. "Traditionally, women were supposed to be confined to the kitchen, that is exploitation. And then they were exploited by the system because it favored men over women." Nashandi recalls the two career options available to women during apartheid were to become a nurse or teacher. Namibian independence was crucial for the people and critical for women.

Nashandi's own story officially began in October 1959 in the village of Ompundja, located in the northern part of Namibia. Born into the apartheid system under heavy South African military control, Nashandi attended one of the two missionary schools that taught English. She remembered how students were harassed, fields were destroyed, community members were arrested, and Namibians were beaten up. In a graphic image, she says, "There were military vehicles with people tied to the exhaust pipes dragging them to death."

Nashandi's school was near a large military base, which meant that the harassment of the students and teachers was a frequent occurrence. "They would come at night and harass us before school started. Then they would go into the classrooms with their weapons and kick out the teachers to disrupt the school. We were so scared." Nashandi and her friends discussed participating in the struggle for independence but staying inside the country was too risky. With a few of her classmates, she escaped by crossing the border to Angola. Out of fear that her family would be harassed, she didn't tell them she was leaving.

Can you imagine having that kind of resolve—not telling your mother you are leaving your family and fleeing the country? When Nashandi mentions this detail, my mind goes to my mother. Momma Sloan, as I affectionately call her, has tracked me down in numerous countries when I simply haven't let her know I've landed safely. "Let your mother know you're safe," echoes in my head whenever I'm overseas. It's a universal sentiment for mothers throughout the world. Nashandi's dedication to protecting her family and the will-power to improve her country is astounding.

Inside Namibia, Nashandi knew women who were educating people about the movement and helping guerrilla fighters by providing food and hiding them from the regime. In 1978, the South Africans launched an airborne attack on the refugee camp organized by the South West Africa People's Organization (SWAPO). Nashandi survived, but some of her friends died, and it motivated her to go and fight. Trained by the People's Liberation Army of Namibia, she joined SWAPO's armed wing unit and fought on the frontlines in the Namibian War of Independence. During that time, she met her future husband. As the war raged, Nashandi got married "in the bush."

Emerging from the shadow of apartheid and fighting for independence were only precursors to a turning point in her journey. While in exile in 1983, Nashandi attended the University of Zambia and got her diploma in youth and development. A year later, she gave birth to her daughter. When her daughter was only ten months old, Nashandi left her with the refugee camp community as SWAPO sent her across the world to campaign for Namibia's independence.

Working as part of the Youth League jumpstarted Nashandi's diplomatic career, as she traveled with the leadership to create awareness and support for her country. They campaigned for education materials, food, and medicine for the refugee camps. Education resources were a top priority, as SWAPO understood they needed to prepare and educate Namibians for independence.

Around this time, the UN recognized SWAPO as the sole, authentic, and legitimate representative of the Namibian people. It had women on all the fronts—political, diplomatic, and military. During the struggle for independence, SWAPO preached equality and gender balance. The mantra, according to Nashandi, was "It's not only men who can fight for independence."

Nashandi was part of a group of men and women who served as SWAPO's earliest diplomats. Before that, she operated as Deputy Representative to the SWAPO Observer Mission to the UN. Securing this leadership opportunity as a young woman gave her the diplomatic skills she would need throughout her career.

There was a UN Council for Namibia during which Nashandi occasionally stood in for her boss and had to "take the floor to speak." Some men around the table would attempt to stop her, as they considered her too young—plus, she was a woman. Diplomatically, she responded, "I know my country better than anybody else. It has nothing to do with age or gender." That said, Nashandi also emphasizes the importance of participation in the conversation. "Women have to participate in the diplomatic field. Women are good at negotiating and can achieve results. You may not always convince a group of people, but you leave them with homework to consider your position."

Namibia gained independence in 1990. As the nation emerged from a period of women exploitation and discrimination, the newly formed government created a gender equality policy. This policy afforded women the opportunity to participate in every field, because the government recognized women as equal contributors to the country's development. The constitution formally guaranteed the rights, freedoms, and equal treatment of women.

The original group Nashandi had worked with in SWAPO and the Youth League helped establish Namibia's Ministry of Foreign Affairs. Many members of that group also became the country's first ambassadors. Nashandi served as Deputy Chief of Protocol and was later appointed as Undersecretary for Political and Economic Affairs. From 1995-1999, she was Namibia's Ambassador to several Scandinavian countries, including Sweden, Norway, Denmark, Finland, and Iceland. Her appointments were based on merit, not merely to fill a quota. "Namibian women do not want to be wheelbarrowed into positions. We want to be appointed on merit or elected democratically. We don't want to be decorating the list," she chuckles.

The U.K. and U.S. are some of the premier postings, according to Nashandi. She says that when she secured both posts, she thought, "Wow, my government really trusts me, as they gave me this responsibility to represent them in these countries."

From 1999-2005, Nashandi served as High Commissioner to the U.K. and Ireland. Her schedule was complicated, as she simultaneously pursued a master's degree in Diplomatic Studies from the University of Westminster. She worked until five o'clock, and classes started at six o'clock and went until half-past ten. She chose not to use the official diplomatic transportation because that would be considered corruption, as her graduate degree was a personal endeavor. Her driver parked the diplomatic car at her home, and then she took the train, which made it a time-consuming journey. Nashandi typically got home around midnight after her two children were already asleep. Her husband was back in Namibia serving as a colonel in the military, so her younger sister joined her in the U.K. to study and help with the family. Nashandi's commitment to her diplomatic studies was resolute.

Nashandi discusses how the Namibian government has emphasized gender equality as a top priority. SWAPO, the ruling party, created a gender equality initiative coined the "zebra policy," which called for 50 percent of leadership positions to be filled by women. Data backs up this approach. After implementing the zebra policy, Namibia saw a massive increase from 26.9 percent women in Parliament in 2009 to 41.3 percent in 2014.[23] U.S. Ambassador to Namibia Lisa Johnson publicly stated in 2019 during International Women's Day, "America needs to follow Namibia's lead and increase women political representation."[24]

In the spirit of Namibia's zebra policy for gender parity, the U.S. could adopt a stars-and-stripes system representing both genders. What if the system also dealt with America's systemic race discrimination? How might this shift the demographics of the U.S. Congress, government, and diplomatic corps? It's compelling to consider the impact of such policies in the United States.

With the zebra policy in full swing, Nashandi ventured back to Namibia from the U.K. and worked in the Office of the President. Before coming to Washington, she was posted as Ambassador to Ethiopia and the Permanent Representative at the African

---

23 Nomkhitha Gysman, "Zebra Listing: A Way Forward for Women," *City Press*, May 7, 2018.

24 Obrien Simasiku, "Namibia Ahead of US in Gender Parity, Admits Diplomat," *New Era Live*, March 25, 2019.

Union (AU). The AU is a very important post, as diplomats lead the charge in regional decisions impacting the African continent. During her time in Ethiopia, Nashandi also represented her country in Djibouti, South Sudan, Sudan, and the UN Economic Commission for Africa. (I thought working full time and writing a book was challenging, but Nashandi's overwhelming list from the Ethiopia post makes my eye twitch.)

Nashandi took an active role helping to develop the African continent when the AU began negotiations for the African Continental Free Trade Area (ACFTA). In terms of the number of countries participating, ACFTA is the largest free-trade area in the world. Of the fifty-five countries, fifty-four signed the agreement as of July 2019. This was of great importance, because the agreement required participating countries to remove tariffs from 90 percent of goods. This opened up access to commodities, goods, and services throughout the continent, and the agreement is estimated to boost intra-African trade by 52 percent by 2022.[25] Nashandi's time in Ethiopia was clearly influential.

Nashandi relates the need for positive trade relationships to promoting peace. "Development does not take place in the midst of war." She asked me, "Who suffers the most during a war?" Before I can respond, the same answer I was going to give leaves her lips: "Women and children." At the AU, discussions are ongoing as to how to fully implement the organization's peace and security architecture. She notes, "Women have to play a role in every field of development. Namibian women have demonstrated that they can do so."

25   Loes Witschge, "African Continental Free Trade Area: What You Need to Know," *Al-Jazeera*, March 20, 2018.

One of the important flagship projects of the AU Agenda 2063 is "Silencing the Guns by 2020." The goal is to end all wars, civil conflicts, gender-based violence, violent conflicts, and prevent genocide in the continent by this year. The initiative's home page features a compelling photo of a woman military member standing strong in a bright green beret. She seems to be in front of a formation of male military members with the social media hashtag "#theAfricaWeWant."[26]

Nashandi says, "These are crucial issues. We have young people leaving the continent, looking for opportunities, and drowning in the Mediterranean Sea. As an African Ambassador, I have to think not only about my country but [also] accelerating the continent's development so that our youth stay and contribute."

Nashandi laughs as she shares that she never dreamed she would be appointed Ambassador to the United States. She thought to herself, "I have to work very hard because I was thrown into this environment." She didn't exactly know where to start. She explains, "The U.S. is a political, diplomatic, and economic jungle. It's huge in size. It's huge in politics. You have to figure out how you're going to navigate and understand the dynamics of what's going on."

Landing in Washington as her country's first woman Ambassador, Nashandi educated herself on American political, economic, and diplomatic systems so that she could do her job. She realized she didn't need to concentrate much on political

---

26 "Silencing the Guns by 2020," African Union, accessed January 15, 2020.

or diplomatic areas but rather on promoting trade and development. "Since the two countries have excellent bilateral relations, I have focused on areas of investment for my country." Promoting Namibia for trade and investments is vital to Nashandi. With its wealth of natural resources, wildlife, and tourism, she sees many opportunities. In fact, Namibia is the only African country eligible to export beef to the U.S. [27]

When I traveled to Southern Africa a few years ago, I remember viewing Namibia's border from the Chobe Forest Reserve and Kasane Forest Reserve on my way to the grand Victoria Falls. There were so many animals! Beautiful Namibian straw bungalows sat on stilts and overlooked the Zambezi River. While the river looked delightful in the heat, I did not take a dip. The safari guide issued a light-hearted, yet serious warning: "It's filled with hippos and Nile crocodiles, which are not cuddly beings."

Nashandi notes that tourism is a great asset to the country. In Washington and around the U.S., she continues to build connections and networks for Namibia. It's a different kind of struggle, bringing investments into her country. A few specific projects include infrastructure development, promoting trade missions, and creating partnerships for business growth.

Nashandi cherishes this responsibility. "Serving my country is not a right, it's a privilege. You have to make sure to promote the country's agenda," she says. "Most of the time I don't think about myself as a woman. I think about myself as a person representing my country. But, at the back of my

---

27 "Namibia Becomes First African Country Eligible to Export Beef to the United States," U.S. Embassy Windhoek, July 13, 2016.

mind, I know I am a woman, who is here, representing other Namibian women. I want other Namibian women to be given the chance to represent the country because we can make equally tangible contributions to our country's development."

According to Nashandi, the nature of diplomacy is being at the table where one hundred ideas can be presented. Diplomacy is sitting around that table to argue and negotiate varying interests. The goal is to navigate those dynamics and find a common position.

March 2020 marks Namibia's 30th anniversary of independence—a milestone of which she is quite proud. With steady confidence, Nashandi states, "I am a mother and a wife, and I continue to represent my country. Nobody can take that away from me."

Promoting Namibia is part of Nashandi's identity. It always has been. Feeling inspired while leaving the Embassy, I couldn't help but hug her.

This book contains multiple stories of diplomats fighting for their countries' independence. The skills and tactics used to solve challenges are applicable to anyone starting from scratch, whether in the private sector, a nonprofit, a social movement, or a life change. Both men and women are driven by the same inner passion or motivation, often finding themselves surprised by the long hours they're able to dedicate to a cause. As the women in these pages demonstrate, determination and resilience are instrumental to any goal; whether working to be "the first" or creating a new initiative, grab your grit and go forth.

CHAPTER 4

THE ROAD TO GENDER PARITY

———

"If you want something said, ask a man; if you want something done, ask a woman."

—MARGARET THATCHER

FIRST WOMAN PRIME MINISTER

OF THE UNITED KINGDOM

As word spread through friends and colleagues that I was writing about diplomacy and women's perspectives, multiple men stepped in and said, "I know someone you must talk to!" These conversations, emails, and phone calls led to many interviews. One friend and colleague from the Austrian Embassy generously connected me to two empowering Austrian diplomats. The act itself—of men allies promoting women colleagues—reminds me of the power of mutual respect and admiration. By continuing to lift each other up, foreign service officers will pave the road to gender parity.

Born in 1944 in the historic city of Vienna, Ambassador Dr. Eva Nowotny is a woman of firsts in the field of diplomacy. She was the first woman officer to enter the Austrian Foreign Service with a doctorate in history, whereas most of her colleagues had degrees in law or international affairs. In speaking over the phone with her while she is on holiday, Nowotny's voice conveys both formality and joyfulness. Her Austrian accent seems to denote the seriousness of her years of diplomatic service.

On a personal note, Austria is quite special to me. It's the first trip I took abroad with my family. We were visiting close family friends who were in Vienna working in the private sector. Memories come flooding back. I recall Momma Sloan wearing her elegant fur coat, the freedom of using public transit without my parents, my friend's school where teachers could bring their dogs to the classrooms, and the warm, sweet smells of the Christmas market. When I moved to Washington, Austria was the first Embassy I visited. Through my work, I helped plan an annual event at the Embassy, which resulted in new friendships with Austrian diplomats. Austria will always hold a special place in my heart. For those reasons and more, the conversation with Nowotny was an honor.

Nowotny's first posting to the U.S. was quite similarly eye-opening. On January 13, 1978, she arrived at JFK airport for a post at the United Nations. She encountered a rude awakening when the security guard examined her identification that was marked for the UN mission. She recalls that the male guard looked at her and asked, "What's a nice girl like you doing at the UN?" That was her first confrontation with public opinion and American attitudes toward women diplomats.

The posting afforded Nowotny political and professional development. She worked directly in the multilateral field, where she was exposed to the "burning issues" such as the Vietnam War, the Soviet invasion of Afghanistan, the Cambodia crisis, the independence of Zimbabwe, and conflicts in the Middle East.

In her deep voice, she recalls several instances in which the impact of women in the field has been especially tangible. The involvement of women in security issues has aided in many UN resolutions. A study that examined eighty-two peace agreements in forty-two armed conflicts between 1989 and 2011 concluded that peace agreements with women signatories are associated with "durable peace."[28] It also stated that peace agreements signed by women show a higher number of provisions aimed at political reform and a higher rate of implementation. The UN has a responsibility to protect and uphold human rights as well as to aid those subjected to human rights violations. Nowotny recalls that in all these international relations situations, "Women were involved in the forefront."

Nowotny was the first woman foreign policy advisor to the head of the Austrian government. "Being in that position was especially exciting given the period," she notes. From 1983 to 1992, she worked through heavy political developments

---

28 Jana Krause, Werner Krause, and Piia Bränfors, "Women's Participation in Peace Negotiations and the Durability of Peace," *International Interactions* 44, no. 6 (2018): 985-1016. August 10, 2018.

in Europe, including the fall of the Berlin Wall, the break-down of the Communist system, and Austria's accession to the European Union. She was also the first woman officer to marry a colleague in the Austrian Foreign Service, and the two have been spotted together throughout the world as they weave their international careers.

Nowotny went on to be the first (man or woman) to hold three ambassadorial postings in a row—in Paris, London, and Washington, D.C. She was also the first woman Austrian Ambassador to all three. Foreign service officers unilaterally agree that these posts are quite strategic and prominent in diplomatic circles. Lastly, as I wrote this book, Nowotny was Austria's first and only woman Ambassador to the U.S. Without planning it, Nowotny has broken barriers and helped pave the way for gender parity.

In 1992, Nowotny arrived to France to find she was the only woman Ambassador in the entire diplomatic corps. "That was quite a shock," she remembers, as Paris had many embassies. It was the early '90s, and many women worked in the diplomatic sector, but she noticed that women were predominately in lower ranks.

Being a woman ambassador was a rarity. However, Nowotny discovered she could turn her unique position into an asset. She stood out among a sea of suited men colleagues, and the public noticed. She used this to her advantage—as she puts it, "being noticed is a very large part of diplomatic work."

Eventually, another woman Ambassador from the U.S. joined Nowotny in Paris. Jokingly, she recalls that in the foreign minister's official speeches to the diplomatic corps, he addressed the esteemed group as "les misters ambassadors," meaning mister ambassadors. Both she and the U.S. Ambassador raised their hands to remind him the group consisted of more than "misters." It was an international learning curve, according to Nowotny. Throughout her professional life, she has encouraged and mentored young women to stand out. She also took a personal interest in helping promote women in the field.

As Board Chair at the University of Vienna, Nowotny spoke in 2019 about how multilateralism—or the alliance of many countries in pursuit of a common goal—is in crisis. As she puts it, "History is shaped by humans, and there are no immutable laws to guide it." She believes that most people will view the current tide of politics or diplomacy as an interruption to a long-term progression. However, she fears that we are, instead, regressing. "Once the social or political trend has taken shape, it forms expectations of all the political and intellectual actors, thus reinforcing the trend and making it difficult to change or reverse. And I fear that might prove true for the decline of multilateral diplomacy."

According to Nowotny, systems and treaties for multilateral diplomacy are deteriorating. It is uncertain whether international leaders will continue to renew strategic pacts that aid in the stabilization of peace. On the other side, countries continue to increase military spending, and the data supports this. In 2018, the Stockholm International Peace Research Institute reported that total world military spending had risen to $1.8 trillion—an increase of 2.6 percent from 2017. Who spends the most? The United States, China, Saudi

Arabia, India, and France. Altogether, their expenditures accounted for 60 percent of global military spending.[29]

Nowotny feels the developments in diplomatic relations over the last twenty-five years have been dramatic. Hierarchical systems of foreign affairs were traditionally under the control of one department and sometimes one government. These systems have broken down and actors have multiplied. This has changed the entire context of foreign relations and diplomatic work.

In her work with both genders on these world issues, Nowotny has found that women are extremely well equipped to deal with the current transitions in politics and diplomacy. She feels women are particularly good at negotiating and willing to share information, as they are less inclined to play power games than male colleagues. "Women tend to be much less hierarchical, to be much better at networking, and sharing information," says Nowotny. She believes these qualities are especially important in diplomacy work today.

Nowotny candidly advises diplomats and politicians to approach everything with an intellectually open mind. Be ready to listen and engage, she says. "Don't get involved in little power struggles and power gains. And, always be as truthful as possible." Nowotny's diplomatic career has taught her that the adage of diplomacy serving to hide what you're thinking while not speaking the truth is "really stupid." Ultimately, a diplomat can *only* achieve results with impartiality,

---

29   "World Military Expenditure Grows to $1.8 Trillion in 2018," *Stockhold International Peace Research Institute*, April 29, 2019.

clarity of thought, and truthful expectations. This wisdom is informed by Nowotny's forty years in diplomacy.

* * *

The road to gender parity in the diplomatic realm is a work in progress. In recent history, I have observed more women in the vortex of dismantling major conflicts and negotiating peace. My mind goes back to August 2014 in the Sinjar Mountains, located in Iraq's disputed territory. Trapped on the mountain, the Yazidis made international headlines as the target of a genocidal campaign by the self-proclaimed Islamic State of Iraq and Syria (ISIS). The Yazidis were singled out in what is known as the "Sinjar massacre." Sadly, this ancient religious minority and ethnic group had long suffered persecution. The images were haunting—families fleeing the area, markets holding women in cages to sell into modern slavery, rolling trucks followed by beheadings. The shocked world watched in what seemed like silence.

Fleeing from ancestral lands is tragically a common occurrence in the region. Both the Yazidi and the Kurdish people have had to move throughout different territories. The Kurds make up the fourth-largest ethnic group in the Middle East.[30] However, they do not have their own country or territory. Spread over Turkey, Iraq, Syria, Iran, and Armenia, the Kurdish people have continually left their homelands throughout history.

---

30   "Who Are the Kurds?," *BBC News*, October 15, 2019.

Bayan Sami Abdul Rahman was eleven years old when she fled Iraq with her family in the mid-1970s. While Rahman is from Sinjar, she is not Yezidi. Nonetheless, her family had to leave. She recounts this experience in an article in *The Telegraph*.[31] "We would be in one village and it would be bombed, so we'd have to flee. One time we lived in an empty school, another time in a shelter for nomads."

Rahman's graceful British accent is reminiscent of her upbringing as a refugee in London. Her late father, Sami Abdul Rahman, participated in the Kurdish freedom movement and served as the General Secretary of the Kurdistan Democratic Party of the Kurdistan Regional Government. Her mother, also an activist and organizer, fought the Kurdish fight in London by opening their home to activists, leaders, political influencers, and opponents of Saddam Hussein's regime.

A large, almost life-size black and white photograph of Rahman's parents hangs in a magnificent frame in her elegant Washington Embassy office. Their traditional Kurdish clothing and confident posture aptly illustrate Rahman's deep roots. Her family played a leadership role for the Kurdish people, and this upbringing seeped into her soul and identity.

After graduating from the University of London, Rahman became a journalist and wrote for the next seventeen years. Others took notice of her work in local London newspapers, and in 1993, she won *The Observer's* Farzad Bazoft Memorial

---

31   Sofia Barbarani, "Meet the Kurdish Female Politician Fighting the Islamic State," *The Telegraph*, February 20, 2015.

Prize. This achievement led her to work for *The Observer* and opened a door at *The Financial Times* (FT). Her reporting for FT in the U.K. and Japan focused on business affairs through the lens of corporations, international trade, and economics. In the 1990s, Rahman was able to visit the Kurdistan Region and started publishing freelance work.

As the world grappled with the fallout from the September 11, 2001 attacks in the U.S., Rahman faced a choice. The U.S. was preparing an invasion of Iraq and she didn't know what that would mean for her homeland of Kurdistan. "Do I want to be, again, looking on from afar as a member of the Kurdish diaspora?" she asked herself then. "Or do I want to be part of the change?"

Rahman consulted with her father, who was serving as Deputy Prime Minister when the U.S. invasion took place. They considered the various possibilities: Rahman shadowing her father, starting an English language newspaper in Kurdistan with British friends and colleagues in media, or finding another way to serve her country. Rahman's friends thought the ideas sounded like "an adventure." But February 1, 2004, changed her world. Her father and brother, along with ninety-six others, were killed in a suicide bombing in Erbil. "I was still in Japan when this happened," she calmly recounts.

Rahman says the terrorist attack focused her mind as a "moment of clarity." She didn't consider a position in diplomacy, but rather, "I just need[ed] to make the jump. I need[ed] to leap from being a member of the Kurdish diaspora." She wanted to serve and help her people more directly in "whatever capacity" possible. Rahman's fluency in both Kurdish and English and her a background in media led to a proposal from the Prime Minister of the Kurdish Regional Government (KRG): "We have representation in London—¬would you consider being the representative?" So, Rahman returned to London—this time, as an "Ambassador without a country," a phrase coined by *The Financial Times*, her old stomping grounds.

With carefully chosen words and sincere humility, Rahman exudes a modest, royal presence. Rahman recognizes that her life is full of contrasts, such as the seriousness of the responsibility to advocate for her people in frivolous settings and at fancy parties. She notes that a diplomat eats and entertains for their country. "It's all part of your work. Hospitality is in the job description of every Ambassador."

Rahman is grateful to fight for her people in highly influential decision-making chambers of the world such as Buckingham Palace, the British Parliament, and leadership receptions. At the same time, she is careful not to let the allure of extravagance distract from her solemn mission—to serve as the voice for the voiceless.

After her post in London as High Representative to the United Kingdom, Rahman came to Washington in 2015 to represent the KRG. I have been a part of multiple audiences to hear her speak on behalf of her people. With a serious tone and sharing factual information, Rahman brings hearts and minds to the fight of the Kurdish people.

Rahman looks around her stately office. The grand floor-to-ceiling drapes spread graciously along the edges of the windows. A delicate chandelier hangs over a prominent wood desk as she shares her story. With hands clasped lightly over her folded legs, she says, "There's an element of this not being real."

In conversations with her husband, she notices the importance of being grounded. Rahman continues to remember the children who have come to Kurdistan with limited educational opportunities due to displacement and fleeing conflict. "When there's even one child who doesn't have a proper education or doesn't have a proper home, I have to remember it is that child that I represent, not this," she affirms, glancing around the grand office. She is proud the Kurdistan Region has a government, that she's in the Leadership Council of one of the parties, and ultimately, that she represents her people.

Despite the outward glamour of the job, Rahman never forgets why she is in the room and at the table. She has a job to do—one of the most challenging jobs compared to her ambassador colleagues. She is tasked with representing a people without an official country. The hill is steep, and sometimes the climb feels insurmountable.

While the KRG was formed in 1992, the region is also making efforts to protect its people with their defense forces, called the Peshmerga. Women are part of the defense forces and have been woven into the tapestry of the society, but according to Rahman, the need for increased women involvement remains. Two of the fourteen representatives like Rahman are women. In the Council of Ministers, there is a special agency called the High Council for Women's Affairs. This agency monitors the government and the legal status of women in Kurdistan and promotes and protects women's rights.

Rahman is a firm believer that women belong throughout the entire governmental process. "I think it is imperative that women are in every level of decision making, not just at the very top, nor just at the bottom or in the middle."

To ensure women participate in Parliament, Iraq maintains a 25 percent quota of women representatives, while Kurdistan's quota is 30 percent. Two separate Parliaments—two separate quotas. During this discussion, Rahman notes that the KRG has three women ministers, which she thinks is the most they have ever had. Unfortunately, she insists, "It's not enough." The number of women ministers is rising in the Kurdistan Region, but the number in Baghdad has decreased. While historically Iraq has had fewer than a handful of women ministers, the current government has zero.

Having women role models in diplomatic spheres throughout the world is important. Rahman points to current role models such as U.S. Secretaries of State Madeleine Albright and Hillary Clinton, U.S. Speaker of the House Nancy Pelosi, and German Chancellor Angela Merkel. The leadership of the KRG respects Chancellor Merkel "enormously." The presence of these women on the world stage helps other countries recognize that women can and should assume leadership roles.

As I write this book, Germany is making waves in women representation. In addition to electing a woman chancellor, Germany's Defense Minister Annegret Kramp-Karrenbauer and German Ambassador to the U.S. Emily Haber are both women. It's important to note that these leaders have also impacted Kurdish society by actively engaging in the fight against ISIS. German forces have trained Peshmerga fighters for this purpose. Rahman stresses the impact of having a woman Defense Minister meet with the Minister of the Peshmerga. "Kurdish society took note. Kurdish leadership took note."

More broadly, Rahman feels the leadership of these high-profile women has made a considerable difference in the Kurdistan Region. "It makes it easier for women like me to be accepted," says Rahman, affirming that this sentiment is shared among other women diplomatic leaders.

Rahman remembers during meetings at the UN and at the State Department in which women were the ones speaking up at the table, demanding action during the ISIS onslaught. Yes, men also took part in the discussions, but Rahman said the women were quite noticeable. Yazidi women also spoke up.

In an impactful plea to the Iraqi Parliament in 2014, Yazidi Kurd member Vian Dakhil called on the Prime Minister to do something. Rahman remembers her saying, "My people are being massacred as we speak and I call on you, I call on the world to do something." Her speech was televised across the world. "I would argue that one of the reasons why President Obama may have ordered the airstrikes on ISIS was probably due to that speech," says Rahman.

While there are very successful and prominent women in Iraq and Kurdistan, Rahman says the region is still very much dominated by men. She is of the opinion that Kurdistan is "more progressive than the rest of Iraq when it comes to women's issues, and maybe some other issues too." However, on the whole, men make all the decisions. Rahman wonders if men consider women in their decision making. After all, she says, Iraq is a country of widows. Both Iraq and the Kurdistan Region have been decimated by genocide and war. "It would be really interesting to know the number of widows in Iraq and the number of female-headed households in a very male-dominated part of the world," she says. A census in Iraq is planned for 2020. This data about heads of households could shift how decisions are made.

In the years of ISIS wreaking violence against Kurdistan, the region flooded with refugees and displaced civilians. Rahman notes that nearly two million people fled to Kurdistan, while its population was five million before the crisis. Oil prices crashed, and Baghdad cut off KRG's budget, which sent the economy into turmoil. The government was forced to significantly reduce salaries. Some Peshmerga fighters in combat with ISIS hadn't been paid for four to five months. Their families didn't have any money.

This is one of the reasons Rahman believes coalitions are vital. "Not burning bridges" and making allies can help Kurdistan. She sees that the diplomatic community is a surprisingly small world, and throughout one's career you run into the same people—"Your worlds collide again." Building a network of allies, especially as a woman, is both individually and collectively important.

Rahman humbly remarks of her leadership, "It's an honor for me, but actually, the bigger honor is to represent that person who doesn't have a voice." Even as the U.S. slowly steps back from supporting KRG as I write this book, Rahman continues her tireless advocacy, and Kurdistan will push forward.

In war and conflict, women are typical targets. A 2014 study estimated that at least one in five women refugees in complex humanitarian settings have experienced sexual violence.[32] How can we enable gender inclusivity and put issues like sexual violence at the forefront of peace agreements and resolutions? A lot of it comes down to language. Gender-sensitive language sets a foundation, but many agreements do not address gender equality or the rights of women whatsoever. For instance, from 1990 to 2018, only 353 of 1,789 agreements (19.7 percent)—including 150 peace processes—had provisions about women, girls, or gender.[33] Language precision is vital in the fight for gender parity, and more women's voices are needed to determine necessary language in agreements.

Comparatively speaking, the foreign ministries in Sweden and the U.S. are closest to gender parity with a 40:60 range of men and women, and the representation of women is rapidly increasing in many other countries.[34] Gender parity in decision making is vital, because when half of the population is excluded, the entire population suffers. As President Barack

---

32 "Report of the Secretary-General on Women, Peace and security," UN Security Council, October 9, 2019. S/2019/800, 2019: 13.

33 "Report of the Secretary-General on Women, Peace, and Security," UN Security Council, October 9, 2019. S/2019/800, 2019: 6.

34 Ann Towns and Karin Aggestam, "The Gender Turn in Diplomacy: A New Research Agenda," *International Feminist Journal of Politics* 21, No.1 (2018): 9-28.

Obama mentioned in a 2019 speech in Singapore, "I'm absolutely confident that for two years, if every nation on earth was run by women, you would see a significant improvement across the board on just about everything . . . [including] living standards and outcomes."[35]

Though violence can be effective, diplomacy is about influencing decisions through nonviolent means—through dialogue, not bloodshed. Through peaceful negotiation of the political, cultural, intellectual, and social, not conflict. With both feminine and masculine voices and a balance of "strong" and "soft" diplomacy. These are the attributes needed around the table. We must build upon the history of diplomacy and continue to fight for gender equality and diversity in all levels of decision making. Just imagine how these changes could shape the next fifty years of international relations.

---

35   Saira Asher, "Barack Obama: Women Are Better Leaders than Men," *BBC News*, December 16, 2019.

PART 2

POWER: VOICES AROUND A TABLE

CHAPTER 5

STRENGTH IN NUMBERS

———

"In a world in which our values are constantly being challenged, we must stand together around ideals that define us."

—ATIFETE JAHJAGA

FIRST WOMAN PRESIDENT OF KOSOVO

While working in Washington, I came across a leader who is making great strides in diplomacy and opening doors for women. She puts the old adage of "strength in numbers" into action and believes that a strong team can overcome any challenge.

It was early spring, and the organization I worked for was hosting an annual diplomacy event. One of the keynote speakers was Irina Bokova, the Director-General of the United Nations Educational, Scientific and Cultural Organization (UNESCO). UNESCO's purpose is to promote international exchanges and partnerships for education, science, culture, human rights, and social justice. The position of Director-General is an honor and a highly-respected role that impacts communities around the world.

Our team waited anxiously as cocktail hour, dinner, and the program were essentially complete. The keynote speaker was late due to a previous event in another state. The infamous traffic of the Northwest corridor stalled the arrival time. While guests routinely leave as soon as desserts are placed on the tables, the opposite happened that evening. Everyone remained happily seated and engaged in conversation as we awaited the arrival of the first woman Director-General of UNESCO.

Customarily in a professional suit with a single strand of pearls, Bokova's traditional appearance is overpowered only by her accomplishments. She speaks French, Spanish, English, Russian, and her mother tongue, Bulgarian. She has represented Bulgaria in many capacities—as Ambassador to France and Monaco, Deputy Minister of Foreign Affairs, Minister of Foreign Affairs ad interim, her country's permanent delegate to UNESCO, and through two terms in Bulgaria's National Parliament. During her tenure in Parliament, Bokova helped draft Bulgaria's new constitution, which eventually led to the country's accession into the EU.

I vividly recall the moment Bokova arrived. A large black bus similar to a band's tour vehicle drove up, and Bokova and her colleague gracefully stepped out and handed a flower bouquet to my coworker, who helped organize the speaking opportunity. A group of us walked down the hallway with Bokova. It reminded me of a crew of paparazzi or reporters following a celebrity side-by-side. Bokova confidently strode to the stage. Her signature angled smile eclipsed the room. Bokova's remarks were short and to the point, yet the room was engulfed by her presence. She had a way of commanding attention. I remember thinking, "Wow." I will hold on to this moment and the feeling of this room. She is a powerhouse.

I reconnect with and interview Bokova a few years later for this book. She has made time in her busy schedule to speak with me over the phone about her foreign service work. She divulges that "I never thought of myself as being a role model. I was just doing my work, my job, what I believe in." She convenes her sense of responsibility when hearing from young women and girls who tell her, "I want to be like you." She continues, "I heard it in Jordan visiting schools, I heard it in Senegal working on projects with young women. I heard it in so many places, if only for that, it was worth it for me going there and talking to them." Bokova is a firm believer in the transcendent power of role models.

Bokova served two terms as Director-General of UNESCO from 2009 to 2017 and was the first woman and the first Southeastern European to hold the position. Afterward, Bokova was among the small group of candidates nominated to replace UN Secretary-General Ban Ki-moon, a position never held by a woman. When she originally joined the foreign service in the '70s, there were not many women. "It was mostly men, but I worked for one particular Ambassador who encouraged me and put a lot of confidence in me," she recalls.

This mentorship was important for Bokova. Women don't always need to seek out women mentors, as both men and women are important for mentorship. This Ambassador assigned important tasks to Bokova and trusted her to write speeches and attend influential conferences. "I think you can feel it when an important responsibility is entrusted to you, and this experience boosted my career," says Bokova. Her experience illustrates how a young professional can flourish and build a reputation early in their career when they are able to gain the trust of leadership and are given more responsibilities.

The spread of democracy in Eastern Europe transformed Bokova's career and opened up the region. "It was a huge opportunity for everybody," Bokova says. The growth of democracy also meant progress for women.

Bokova recalls that before democracy, women in Eastern Europe still had opportunities for education. She remembers women participating in the academic and legal sectors in particular. However, in other countries, women did not have those options. The access afforded by democracy created a space for women to participate in diplomacy, political involvement, and leadership. Bokova explains, "It was kind of a revolution, no doubt about it." The democratization of Eastern Europe led to many more women leading in foreign ministries.

Early in her career, Bokova advocated for diplomacy at the United Nations, where she was responsible for social, legal, and women's affairs. She participated in UN conferences for women's empowerment and equality. In 1980, she attended her first big meeting for the UN in Copenhagen on women's empowerment and equality.

Bokova recalls that experience vividly. "I will never forget when I saw such strong women diplomats participating in debates. I remember diplomats and women ambassadors from Australia, the Philippines, Egypt, and other African countries. I was very impressed and thought that maybe one day, I could become like them."

Bokova's early experience at the UN led her to her ultimate passion for facilitating multilateralism and multiculturalism. According to her, they are the ideals for which every diplomat should strive.

While she attended many large conferences in her professional capacity, Bokova recalls one that stood out in particular. This was the famous 1995 World Conference on Women in Beijing where First Lady Hillary Clinton said, "If there is one message that echoes forth from this conference, it is that human rights are women's rights . . . and women's rights are human rights." That conference and the speech put women's rights in perspective, and Bokova thinks back on it often, stating, "[It] was the peak of so many years of aspirations."

For Bokova, the '90s were transformative as the "romantic" years of democracy in Europe and everywhere. "There was the feeling that we were moving towards the global common good. This common good was also the beginning of gender equality," she remembers. She believes there was more unity around the ideas of democracy and gender equality at that time.

In her recent leadership roles, Bokova has attended meetings where she will enter the room and men will ask, "Are you the interpreter?" or outright assume so. Stereotyping happens often, according to Bokova. During our conversation, she thinks back to the responses from senior colleagues when she was the first woman elected as Director-General of UNESCO. Sarcastically, she tells me she received a few "nice" messages from the senior management team who were international directors. One in particular said, "Director-General, you actually did quite well today during the meeting." Bokova says this one stuck with her. "They wanted to congratulate me, but it was indeed condescending. I ignored it. As long as you believe in what you're doing and have strong convictions, you ignore it and move on."

Bokova chose to focus her attention on her work rather than the patronizing messages. She recounts a visit to Kabul, Afghanistan, where she helped promote one of the largest literacy programs for the country. She wanted to visit a certain village, but the military told her she couldn't go due to security measures. Rather than let this roadblock stop her, Bokova organized for the young women and their children to be brought to Kabul. She wanted to find out what they learned from the program, why it was important to them, and whether the husbands of the families supported the literacy programs.

One woman told Bokova, "Our husbands are supportive, but they're illiterate. They don't have time to go learn, as they are always working, and we come from a small village." At the end of their meeting, one of the women asked Bokova, "Could you please organize such courses for our husbands?" The power of the literacy program was touching for Bokova, and the meeting was something she will always remember.

The Women, Peace, and Security (WPS) Agenda, established by the UN, recognizes "women not only as recipients of aid or justice, but also as agents, integral to peace, stability, and security."[36] Bokova's work is a living testament to this philosophy; her career underlines the essential role of women uniting to work in conflict prevention, management, and resolution.

Bokova firmly believes that women need to support women. A successful woman is not truly successful if other women are not. "Being clever or talented is not enough," she believes, unless you share support and opportunities. When she was elected to her position at UNESCO, Bokova saw that the management and leadership of the organization needed to change. She recalls that when she arrived at her position, around 23 percent of leadership positions were held by women. She made a point to appoint qualified women as half of her team.

"Women should not be present just for a quota, they should be given a space to show what they can do," Bokova asserts. Being a mentor to younger women was crucial during Bokova's leadership. She attributes her growth to strong mentorship, and that experience paved the way for her to do the same, enabling others to grow. When she left her role at UNESCO, around 50 percent of director-level and higher leadership positions were held by women.

In essence, a critical mass is of utmost importance to Bokova. People need to see that women can do the jobs, which leads to culture change and is imperative for growth

---

36 "Gender & Disarmament Resource Pack for Multilateral Practitioners," The United Nations Institute for Disarmament Research (UNIDIR), January 2019.

in gender equality around the table. Toward the end of our call, Bokova stresses the importance of putting yourself on the side—"to understand the why, fears, and concerns." Using the ability to listen is of "utmost importance." Many diplomats emphasize the importance negotiations and dialogue. However, the ability to listen is the foundation for ultimately being heard.

In the UN and the global context, Bokova is concerned that politics and diplomacy have become more brutal and macho. She feels diplomacy is becoming sidelined, and the women's agenda is slipping away from changing geopolitics. "This worries me, and I hope I'm not right," she says. "If we start parceling and fragmenting the world, it's very dangerous. Where would we go from there?" Bokova believes that the international community is stronger when we educate people in an atmosphere where "we understand at the end of the day, we are all human beings."

* * *

Establishing guiding principles is the first step toward most social change. Next come the numbers to amplify and validate those principles. To gain momentum for gender parity, we need more people pushing the principle.

Vlora Çitaku understands this idea personally. She and I meet in a building off K Street in Washington, where an office space serves as the Embassy of Kosovo. We sit opposite one another at a long wooden table with red chairs and geometric art prominently illuminating the white walls. With striking high cheekbones and coffee-colored eyes, Çitaku's grace is matched by the sincere gravity of representing her country.

Çitaku was born on October 10, 1980, in former Yugoslavia, a time of turmoil in the region. She witnessed constant police and military presence on the streets, her parents losing their jobs, and the violent assault of her teachers. "As a child, I realized that freedom is a precondition for the creation of any other value. If you're not free, you cannot be anything," she says with conviction.

As a teenager during the outbreak of the Kosovo War, Çitaku became an interpreter and ad hoc contributor for Western news outlets. Serbian military forces soon came to deport her family from their home as part of the ethnic cleansing campaign. Her parents sent her and her three sisters to Macedonia for safety. As she carried her little sister in her arms, Çitaku and her siblings became refugees overnight.

The Kosovo War started in late February 1998 and lasted until early June 1999. Under the leadership of President Bill Clinton and U.S. Secretary of State Madeline Albright, the United States and its NATO allies took action by bombing Serbian forces and infrastructure responsible for the atrocities. Although the action was not sanctioned by the UN and was considered illegal under some interpretations of international law, Secretary Albright maintains that it was the right thing to do.[37] After the war, the

---

37 David Greene, "Albright: U.N. Needs To Show Its Relevance On Syrian Issue," *Morning Edition*, NPR, September 26, 2013.

Kosovo memory book database documented that more than 13,500 people were killed or went missing during the conflict.[38] Between 1.2 to 1.5 million Kosovar Albanians were displaced.[39]

As the U.S. helped to end the war, Çitaku and her sisters returned to their war-torn country and reunited with their parents. From 1999 to 2000, Çitaku joined the provisional government of Kosovo as Chief of Protocol and became a political party spokesperson. She says that, "For me and my generation, being politically active was a way of survival."

In 2002, Çitaku began her studies at the University of Prishtina while serving two terms as a delegate to the Kosovo Assembly until 2007. The year 2007 was a busy one for Çitaku. She earned her master's degree from the Kosovo Institute for Journalism and Communication, served as the head of the Kosovo Communications Working Group of the Unity Team under the president, and *then* became Deputy Foreign Minister. Wow.

Çitaku helped draft the first package of laws while serving as one of the youngest members of Parliament. "I'm not sure what's worse, being young or being a woman?" Çitaku asks rhetorically. Laughing, she adds, "Now imagine being both."

---

38 Nataša Kandić, Patrick Ball PhD, and Michael Spagat, "Kosovo Memory Book Database," National Library "Pjetër Bogdani," Prishtina, February 4, 2015.

39 Heike Krieger, "The Kosovo Conflict and International Law: An Analytical Documentation 1974-1999," Cambridge University Press (2001): 90, accessed January 18, 2020.

Kosovo created a quota that at least 30 percent of the members of the Parliament had to be women.

Some of the first laws discussed were the rights and privileges of the president. The language of the law started with "the president and the first lady" and followed that wording throughout. "Subconsciously, the experts who drafted the law always thought of the president as a man," Çitaku remembers. Çitaku raised her hand and the speaker gave her the floor. In a straightforward manner, she said, "The language of the law is sexist. It should be 'the president and the spouse' because we will have a woman president one day." Laughter exploded throughout the chamber. The speaker scoffed, "Vlora, you're so ambitions. You have to wait." Çitaku pressed on and encouraged members to vote on the amendment to the language. She repeated, "This is not funny. The language is sexist. Let's vote on the amendment and move on."

A few years later, Çitaku felt proud as Kosovo elected the first woman president in southeastern Europe. Sitting with me now, she smiles and says, "Guess who laughed back?"

February 17, 2008, marks the day Kosovo declared independence. Çitaku realized the enormity of the situation. She thought of the generations who had fought and sacrificed so much. She felt the magnitude of the honor and privilege to be a part of history and shape her country. She thought about her mother who had lost eleven members of her family in the war. On the day of the declaration, her mother came to her and said, "Now the burden is in your hands. It's up to you and your generation to make it succeed or fail."

In recounting this with me, Çitaku starts, "It was the most memorable moment in my life. I could feel the heartbeats of my uncles and . . . ," but her voice trails off as she tears up. She pauses to gain composure. At this point in our conversation, I have to look at her nose as I can also feel tears welling in my eyes. Even listening to the playback of our conversation catches my breath with emotion.

Çitaku recalls sitting in the first row of the parliamentary chambers as the actual declaration document sat around five steps away. "Those five steps were the longest steps of my life. I had an out-of-body experience."

From 2007 to 2009 she served as Deputy Foreign Minister and from 2009 to 2010 as Acting Foreign Minister. As she began her role as Deputy Foreign Minister, she had nothing in her office except a chair. Really—I ask her twice to confirm. "We had to build everything from scratch. The physical infrastructure, the legal infrastructure, human resources, and policies." Çitaku has had to accomplish all these things while confronting the adversity of gender.

To that end, Çitaku recalls decorating her ministerial office wall with photos of women from Kosovo and Albania who inspired her. Whenever she was feeling down, disappointed, or underappreciated, she would sit down next to the wall with a coffee and look at the photos. The wall reminded her that no matter how challenging her situation was, the women staring back at her—pioneers in their own right— had faced far more difficulty. She understood it was her job to continue and make it easier for women who might follow her.

From 2010 to 2014, Çitaku was the Minister of European Integration, and she also served as Chief Negotiator of Kosovo to the European Union from 2013 to 2014. She fondly remembers Catherine Ashton, who served as the inaugural High Representative of the Union for Foreign Affairs and Security Policy (basically the EU's foreign policy chief). Along with Ashton, the U.S. Secretary of State at the time was Hillary Clinton.

Çitaku describes this as "a very unique dynamic. We were all women. I saw firsthand how women empowered one another in dealing with the Western Balkans. It led to the most sustainable progress that we have seen in the region." Why was the woman-led team successful? They secured the first major agreement between Kosovo and Serbia and the historic Stabilization and Association Agreement. Although a few EU countries still do not recognize Kosovo, these agreements were crucial for the stabilization of the Western Balkans.

Çitaku argues for the importance of alliances and allies to push any agenda forward. She describes how women trailblazers are judged when they succeed or fail, as the outcome gets equated to the gender as a whole. However, the same correlation isn't made when a man fails. That's one of the reasons why, according to Çitaku, there's an elevated sense of responsibility to succeed.

Çitaku compares a woman politician's success to a grading system—that as a woman in politics or government, you essentially have to be an A+ student to get a C-. The expectations and standards for women are different, and the pressure is enormous, but the feeling of success is unmatched.

There's a deep sense of satisfaction to be found in helping build your country—that's the reward, Çitaku says. "My experience working with women is that success is never a selfish project."

Throughout her career, Çitaku has worked to increase women representation, whether in her government, the Ministry of Foreign Affairs, or various embassies. She suggests keeping a "list" of women pioneers and leaders in different fields, in order to debunk the myth among men that there are not enough qualified women or that women don't want certain roles. That's when she hands any naysayers "the list."

Çitaku says to "Always make sure you create room for other women. Help one another. Empower one another. Nothing can be accomplished alone. Sustainable change requires a critical mass of people. You need more voices around the table."

Before coming to Washington, Çitaku served as Kosovo's Consul General in New York from 2014 to 2015. The year 2015 marked another pivotal moment when she officially became Kosovo's Ambassador to the U.S. "Presenting credentials" is a formal ceremony in which foreign ambassadors personally appear before the head of state of their assigned country. It officially marks the start of the ambassadorship, and there's an obligatory photo op.

Çitaku laughs as she tells me about the day. She was in her bathroom, doing her hair and makeup to prepare for the ceremony. Her phone rang. It was her uncle who survived the war. He didn't call very often, so she picked up. He began, "Vlora, I called to remind you of a story."

She paused—it was not the best day to catch up with her uncle in the midst of preparing for this momentous occasion. But she politely encouraged her uncle to go on. "You were six years old and one summer you told me, 'Uncle, next summer, I'm going to America and I'm going to talk to the president. I know he will save us.'"

Çitaku had forgotten the story completely. Emotion filled her, and she reflected while making sure her mascara didn't run. Hearing this anecdote felt like a destiny fulfilled: "A six-year-old child in a forgotten place had hope because America existed. I am one of the very few who had the opportunity to be a part of something far bigger and far more important than myself."

In reflecting on this, Çitaku adds that not all people can reach what society deems to be ultimate success. "Not all of us will have great careers, become millionaires, or be famous. Aim high and work hard, but don't be disappointed. There are circumstances above our reach that determine things. But you should always do your best."

Çitaku attributes her professional progression to her strong mother and supportive father. She says her family pushed her and gave her wings. "I try to work hard and make my mom proud because it's women like her who paved the way for me."

Çitaku's mother was born in a remote village on top of a mountain, where she walked for two hours each day to get to school. She was the first woman of her village and region to attend university. She also fought for the emancipation of women throughout her entire life. Çitaku's mother was always politically active, and she still teaches at a university. "She is the smartest and bravest person I have ever met. She's an inspiration to women from my country and Albania," said Çitaku. She carries a central lesson from her mother: do what you want, but whatever you choose, do it with love and dignity.

People sometimes ask Çitaku what she is afraid of. She still says, "My mom." Çitaku speaks with her mother every day. "I could never live with letting her down. I still haven't fulfilled my mom's request—Kosovo is still in the making," she concludes.

While Çitaku continues to rise in her career, she repeatedly finds that "Strong women and women in positions of power are still considered exotic creatures. To make it sustainable and the norm, we need more women around the table." Strength in numbers is essential. With more voices around the table to represent the diversity of their communities, we will be stronger as individual nations and citizens of the world.

CHAPTER 6

COALITION AND CONSENSUS BUILDERS

———

"To make peace, one must be an
uncompromising leader. To make peace,
one must also embody compromise."

—BENAZIR BHUTTO

FIRST WOMAN PRIME MINISTER OF PAKISTAN AND THE
FIRST WOMAN ELECTED TO LEAD A MUSLIM STATE

In the sweltering July heat, I rush to meet with Hungary's first woman Ambassador to the United States, Dr. Reka Szemerkényi, at the Center for European Policy Analysis (CEPA). She calmly greets me and walks me into her office adorned with awards on her bookshelf.

When learning about her background, I found that she was awarded the Slovak Atlantic Commission's award "In Appreciation of Promoting Freedom and Security in Central Europe" in 2013, the "Bene Merito" honor by Radoslaw Sikorski from the Ministry of Foreign Affairs of Poland in 2010, the L'Ordre National du Mérite Commandeur by President Jacques Chirac 2001, and the National Service Award for her contribution to Hungary joining NATO by the Minister of Defense of Hungary in 1999. An impressive diplomat, no doubt.

Dr. Szemerkényi has a gracious smile and chestnut eyes, and she is seated in a navy-blue suit with gold embellishments. Her presence and unpretentious parlance put you at ease and say nothing of her impressive intellectual background. Szemerkényi earned her PhD summa cum laude in economic history from Hungary's Pázmány Péter Catholic University, and she completed her master of Strategic Studies as a Fulbright Fellow at Johns Hopkins University School of Advanced International Studies (SAIS) in Washington. She also has a master of International Relations from the Institut Européen des Hautes Études Internationales in Nice, France, and from ELTE University Budapest. Lastly, Marymount University in Arlington, Virginia, and the National Public University of Hungary awarded her an honorary Doctor of Humane Letters.

Szemerkényi opens our discussion with a universally shared opinion: "It is a common feeling of many women in diplomacy that we are the only women around the table." In Europe, Szemerkényi's work in security policy has been in an exclusively male environment. Her journey did not start in security policy, however, but in international relations and diplomacy.

During the move from communism to democracy and capitalism in the early 1990s, and after the regime change,

Szemerkényi was offered a position with the Hungarian Ministry of Defense. She noticed the majority of the Ministry of Defense consisted of "soviet trained military guys" with few civilians and no women besides cleaning crews and secretaries.

It was in this environment that Szemerkényi discovered a library in the basement of the Ministry of Defense. She explored shelves of dusty "classified" books about international relations that had been translated into Hungarian. "It was ridiculous," she says. While it was completely normal for most international relations students to have access to these books, for her it was a shocking, new discovery. "What's the difference between neutrality and nonalignment? Even some security policy concepts were classified by the Soviet Union," she recalls.

Szemerkényi worked during the day, and at night, she educated herself on elements of international relations and conflict. As she consumed the unearthed knowledge, she realized her real interest was not just in diplomacy, but specifically security policy. This discovery gave her passion and direction.

From 1998 to 2002, Szemerkényi served as the Hungarian State Secretary for Foreign Policy and National Security Advisor to the Prime Minister of Hungary Viktor Orbán. She notes, "The field of security policy is a field of conflicts: potential and future, present and past." During our conversation, Szemerkényi emphasized the need for both men and women around the table. "[Security policy] is about disagreements, it's about tense situations, it's about issues that are contradictory by nature. So, both genders are needed."

The Prime Minister tasked Szemerkényi with the responsibility of drafting the cybersecurity strategy and law for Hungary within a two-year time frame. This was a huge undertaking, as many stakeholders in finance, security, and defense were involved.

Most of the government officials had never met each other. According to Szemerkényi, "They were sending messages, emails, and materials, and there wasn't a closeness of alignment [among] the various positions." Rather than creating a consensus of commonly accepted text or a strategy, Szemerkényi soberly explains, "We were killing each other's versions."

Within the short timeline, she invited all stakeholders to gather in person at the prime minister's office. "That's when the group realized they had never actually met," she recalls.

She had everyone sit down around the same table, look at one another in the eyes, and communicate on the complex security strategy. In looking back at everyone seated in the same room around the table, she says the "magic of sitting together can create an atmosphere." It created an openness for coalition building. Creating clearer lines of communication allowed the group to draft the language of the national cybersecurity strategy. The plan was then presented and accepted by the Hungarian Parliament, ultimately becoming law.

A year later, Szemerkényi represented Hungary at the European Union's inaugural high-level Cybersecurity Conference. She shared Hungary's national security strategy on establishing a cybersecurity practice. After the presentation, she noticed the screen above the head of the commission. The headline read "Hungary presents best practice to European Union."

"Women have a more natural talent for approaching conflict compared to men," according to Szemerkényi, but "a combination of men and women is hugely important, because in many cases, what is missing is an ability to smooth things together."

* * *

In an undisclosed office off of K Street, an elevator takes me directly into the Embassy of Saint Kitts and Nevis. The floor is shared with Saint Vincent and the Grenadines. I sit down with Ambassador Dr. Thelma Patricia Phillip-Browne around a circular wooden table over a striped carpet. She is adorned with beaded jewelry, and her disposition is cordial and peaceful. Educated and trained in the medical field, Phillip-Browne was appointed Ambassador in 2015 and credentialed in 2016. She shares with a laugh, "I was born in a house that was smaller than this room."

Phillip-Browne came from a very poor working-class family with eight surviving children. Her mother had a basic primary school education and stressed the importance of learning by pushing the eldest son to attend secondary school. Unfortunately, she passed away when Phillip-Browne was only eleven. Her father was working in the Virgin Islands at the time. Her eldest brother took charge of the family and encouraged education amongst the siblings. Her brother remembered that Phillip-Browne was interested in nursing, but the sciences were only taught to men and not at the all-girl high school. When the all-boys and all-girls schools merged, fourteen-year-old Phillip-Browne sat in her first science class.

With only two years before the final school exams, she found catching up "challenging," but was successful. Phillip-Browne decided to take chemistry in preparation for medical school. However, she missed the final practical and college scholarship exams due to a scheduling mix-up. Fortunately, she was able to take the French and English exams to secure a scholarship. She succeeded, which allowed her to enter college and study whichever discipline she wanted. Phillip-Browne received the Princess Alice Scholarship along with another student. She says, "It was fate; I wouldn't have done as well on the chemistry exam. Taking the French and English exams allowed me to get the scholarship." Through the University of the West Indies, Phillip-Browne earned her medical degree and later specialized in dermatology at the University of Wales in Cardiff. She also earned a master of Theology from Anderson University.

Phillip-Browne admits, "I don't really like politics. I think it can be divisive and destructive. I got involved in politics at a crucial time." During polarized times in her country, she wrote articles to share her concerns. Her husband, a lawyer, was politically active as well. Phillip-Browne says that in most cases, people were supported by the government in some shape or form. However, doctors, lawyers, and people in business were able to voice their political views because they weren't dependent on government subsidies.

She shares that in the Caribbean, women play a very strong role in the family and as top civil servants. However, they tend to shy away from politics, as they are heavily scrutinized compared to men. Phillip-Browne helped author part of the health portion for an election platform. However, due to concerns about corruption, she left politics and went into private medical practice. She said to one of the parliamentarians, "If you ever start a revolution, call me."

When the Team Unity party alliance formed, Phillip-Browne decided to align herself accordingly. They had all men candidates, so she and a few other women spoke on the platform. When the party was elected in 2015, the Prime Minister inquired whether she wanted to serve as an Ambassador. She was sent to Washington in September 2015; however, she was not officially credentialed until January 2016 due to a hurricane in the region, which prevented her from getting her documents from Barbados.

In addition to gender in politics and diplomacy, Dr. Phillip-Brown addresses ageism. "Women get better after our best-buy or sell-by date." She explains, "If you go to a supermarket shelf, you'll see items with a sell-by or best-by date. The implication is that after that date, things start to deteriorate. Traditionally, there's a perspective of women that you raise children and you get to menopause, then after menopause you are on the decline." I pause with my mouth open, waiting on what she is going to say next.

She says that there's also less pressure now on women to get married compared to when she was younger. Regardless, "after raising children and a family, women can put that behind them and devote time to something else. With that experience, women have a broader grasp of life that they are able to contribute, so it's like they have a second wind or a second act." Phillip-Browne believes that all women, no matter their age, can contribute.

She serves in the Caribbean Community and Common Market (CARICOM) Caucus of Ambassadors. A group of twenty Caribbean countries comprise CARICOM and focus on regional integration. It includes fifteen Member States and five Associate Members. As a group, the ambassadors representing these countries engage with the U.S. State Department and members of Congress to build coalitions and consensus on important issues for the region.

In 2016, President Obama signed into law H.R.4939, or the U.S. Caribbean Strategic Engagement Act. It was a bipartisan effort that led to the creation of a plan called Caribbean 2020. Phillip-Browne tells me about the plan's six pillars—security, diplomacy, prosperity, energy, education, and health.

She says, "One of my first challenges was to get health and education included. Health, in a sense, is not just the absence of disease, but also mental, physical and spiritual well-being. If you don't have a healthy and educated population, you won't have prosperity or security."

The Caucus examined the responsibilities of various countries in CARICOM along with the expertise of the ambassadors dividing up the pillars, so each area has a chairperson leading the issue area. Since Phillip-Browne is a doctor—and her country has had prime ministers who have been doctors who had retained the health portfolio—she became responsible for the health pillar.

While the U.S. seems to want to focus on security and energy, Phillip-Browne continues to push the health agenda. She asserts, "If you don't have a healthy and educated population, all these things suffer. For instance, crime is a public health issue and it really started with the drug trade."

It's challenging for Caribbean islands to police themselves with their many little ports and beaches. Phillips-Browne says, "We are small islands in the deep blue sea, confronting two devils. Drugs coming from the South satisfy the appetite in the North and guns coming from the North go to the South." The drug trade has been a challenge for the region, but according to Phillip-Browne, it has been improving.

To paint a complete picture, she dives deeper into the crux of the issue—the complex link between drugs, crime, and public health. In 1992, the U.S. Surgeon General Everett Koop declared violence a public health emergency. In 1993, American health ministers approved a joint resolution proclaiming violence prevention a public health priority.

However, Phillips-Browne says such measures missed the point. "It did not get the traction that it deserved . . . it was criminalized rather than looked at as a public health issue." She mentions how someone convicted of crack cocaine possession was sentenced to longer punishments than someone with powder cocaine. While the chemical difference between the substances is small (crack cocaine is mixed with baking soda), crack cocaine was prominently used in poor, typically Black communities, while powder cocaine was predominantly used in white communities. "It's one of the reasons there are so many Black people incarcerated in the U.S.," she commented.

Phillip-Browne continues, "All drug abuse is classified as mental illness. I'm trying to get the State Department to reconsider the social dimensions and determinants of crime. Poverty, drug abuse, and poor education are all connected. Both the Caribbean and the U.S. need to recognize health and education as the social determinants of crime, which is a public health issue."

She tells me about the CDC-Kaiser Permanente Adverse Childhood Experiences (ACE) Study. It is one of the largest investigations of childhood abuse, neglect, and household challenges and discovers how those situations lead to later-life health and well-being.[40]

Between 1995 to 1997, more than 17,000 Health Maintenance Organization (HMO) members from Southern California who received physical exams completed confidential surveys about their childhood experiences, current health status, and behaviors. The surveys found that early adversity factors such as abuse, neglect, and other trauma had lasting impact in the form of health issues—including depression, anxiety, unintended pregnancy, HIV or STDs, cancer, diabetes, alcohol and drug abuse, education, occupation, and income.[41]

---

40   "About the CDC-Kaiser ACE Study," Centers for Disease Control and Prevention, updated April 2, 2019.

41   Ibid.

"This study crossed race and class. [It determined that] if children are exposed to four or more factors, their brain development and reasoning are impaired, which in turn influence decisions on health, education, and social situations." Phillip-Browne continues to build coalitions and consensus to make an impact in this area.

She also discusses how climate change is a major issue for her country and has built sea walls to combat rising water levels. "I tell our partners all the time—if you're on an island and there's a hurricane bearing down on you, you can't evacuate. We are human beings so we can't evaporate. So, we have to educate, innovate, agitate, and advocate."

She poignantly notes, "We share one planet . . . We have a mind, body, and spirit. If we see the world from that perspective, we will treat each other differently. Part of it is that we see each other as 'us' and 'them,' whether due to religion, race, or economics. There's a lot of fear of each other. As we deal with each other, we have to dispel those fears," she says.

During the time of our interview, the coronavirus is sweeping throughout the world. Phillip-Browne recounts that on her way to the Embassy that morning, she told her driver, "Sometimes things like the viruses come to remind us that it doesn't matter where we are born, what color we are, or the religious beliefs we have. It's an equalizer. We need to pull together the same kind of energy [for] saving or sustaining our common humanity. It's unfortunate that it takes these kinds of things for us to come to this realization."

Phillip-Browne's consensus building is at the center of everything she says or does. During a CSPAN broadcast of a panel hosted by the Center for Strategic and International Studies (CSIS), she eloquently communicated that in the tapestry of the universe, we each have a purpose. "Some of us may be a black thread, some white, some pink, some purple. Every one of us has a unique slot in that tapestry. As long as we find that slot and are the best little color we can be, then we can enhance the whole tapestry and those around us can make us shine. Find your slot, be the best you can be, and enhance the tapestry of the universe."[42]

* * *

There are many people involved in diplomatic work in nontraditional ways. The military often plays a diplomatic role when securing regions or negotiating security efforts. U.S. Army Major General Linda Singh is one example of those people. She was the first African American and woman to lead Maryland's National Guard. Having worked in both the private and government sectors, she has served the military in both enlisted and officer roles for more than thirty years. She shares that being able to lead the organization that originally "saved her life" has been a motivational force. When she was seventeen, joining the military "took her off the streets."

With her dark hair pulled back tight in military fashion with deep brown eyes, Singh is straightforward, concise, and at the same time, genuinely kind and caring about the people

---

42 The Center for Strategic and International Studies, "Global Perceptions of the U.S.," CSPAN video, 1:19:30, January 16, 2018.

she led. Her command staff also happened to be the first in the U.S. to consist of all women. She attributes this to talent and nothing more. In 2015, only 7.1 percent of U.S. military generals and admirals were women.[43]

As the Commander of the Maryland National Guard, Singh served as a senior advisor to the Governor of Maryland in the cabinet responsible for "the readiness, administration, and training of more than 6,700 members of the Military Department."[44] The 2015 Baltimore protests and civil disturbance made headlines across the U.S. and globally from the outpouring following the death of Freddie Gray, a twenty-five-year-old African American man who perished due to injuries during an arrest. During the protests, around twenty police officers were injured, 250 civilians arrested, and 350 businesses damaged. Thousands of police, in tandem with the Maryland National Guard, were deployed under a state of emergency.[45]

I remember watching the TV coverage of Baltimore citizens marching in the streets. I recall the fires and the riot police. In Washington, D.C., and other cities around America, people marched and protested in support of Baltimore. It was a heart-wrenching and tense time.

43   Katherine Kidder, Amy Schafer, Phillip Carter, and Andrew Swick, "From College to Cabinet: Women in National Security," Center for a New American Security, February 2017.

44   "Major General Linda L. Singh," Maryland Global Initiative for Cybersecurity, University of Maryland, accessed December 2019.

45   Yvonne Wenger, "Damage to Businesses from Baltimore Rioting Estimated at About $9 Million," *The Washington Post*, May 13, 2015.

"Just having my voice in the room with some of the males around me allowed me to bring a very different perspective," Singh shares candidly. She recalls asking the group, "How do we deescalate things in a way that still moves towards a solution, that makes sense for the overall team?" When she used the idea of "the team," she included citizens of Baltimore in particular, because she wanted to bring them in as part of the solution. She was thinking like a military leader, not solely as a woman. "It just so happened that in many cases, I was the only woman in the room or one of a few," she remembers.

At the time, Singh's mind kept going to the fabric of society—made of mothers, parents, sisters, brothers, children. She chose to use those perspectives to help connect the military to a higher level of decision-making. Allowing peaceful protests while controlling the agitators was challenging, to say the least, and the team needed to address the problem from different angles to find a solution. She says that if "you're trying to jam something through a hole that was not even designed for the size of the peg that you're pushing it through," it's not going to work. Having both men and women helps to balance the perspectives of a problem and find a solution. Building coalitions and consensus during tense and violent times is diplomatic work and is something Singh has done throughout her career.

Singh's deployment to Afghanistan was a pivotal point in her life. It was during "a very contentious environment where you never knew what was going to happen on any given day." The only outlet was exercise or reading. She jokes, "You can't just go off into the city and go shopping, right? It's a very limited environment."

Sharing 12x12-foot living quarters gives a person a certain appreciation for things. Singh worked in an operational role using both her military and civilian skills to communicate diplomatically with the Afghans.

During her deployment, Singh's team lost a service member, and the impact was tremendous. "When you have to go through that, you have to be able to deal with it as you have to go back to work. Your job doesn't stop because that happened," she reflects.

This experience taught Singh how to personally cope with loss on a deeper level. That experience allowed her to release emotions she had harbored from her past. The release lifted an internal struggle and ultimately led to a personal transformation.

Being a woman in a "security environment" can be challenging. She found that oftentimes, other women would look up to her and ask, "How did you get to that position?" They, too, want promising careers. They want to lead. They want to make a difference in society. "You see this happening time and time again where the women are just wanting to have role models in this environment," Singh says.

During our interview, Singh tells me her three takeaways of effective leadership from the military—the importance of being out in public, being visible, and ultimately, being accessible. Singh is glad to have been a part of senior leadership through her work with other countries. In addition to developing an impressive skill set, she served as a role model for other women in nations where they hadn't seen women senior leaders.

According to Singh, the presence of women for peacekeeping "positively affects aspects of local populations' interactions and perceptions" of the operation.[46] She calls her mindset "the art of the possible." This mantra has allowed her to determine how to move forward and shape the future of society.

Researchers have found that "more diverse military organizations, including some of the nation's most elite forces engaged in combat operations in Iraq and Afghanistan, perform better on the battlefield because of the innovative approaches to problem-solving that more diverse teams bring."[47] Both research and reality demonstrate that more women are needed in top leadership positions for national security and in the private sector.

Working in a predominantly male-infused field, Singh found herself in situations that were usually "95 percent male-dominated." According to "Her Power Index" by *Foreign Policy* magazine, women make up one-third of the U.S. foreign policy staff as of 2018, which is much less than the 47 percent of women who make up the country's workforce.[48] Whether in foreign policy or military leadership, more women are needed for effective consensus building.

---

46 Katherine Kidder, Amy Schafer, Phillip Carter, and Andrew Swick, "From College to Cabinet: Women in National Security," Center for a New American Security, February 2017.

47 Ibid.

48 "How the U.S. Government Is Failing Women in Foreign Policy," The Her Power Index, *Foreign Policy*, October 15, 2019.

Singh says that her male colleagues didn't tokenize her because she built a level of respect and trust. She goes into any situation and uses a key tool: listening. She claims, "Women tend to be really good listeners." She then asks strategic questions that allow the group to work through their answers and walk through the problem. Singh is of the opinion that teams learn best this way as opposed to being given the answers, because they arrive at a consensus on their own. She says she can only cultivate that process if she's actively listening, summarizing, and asking the right questions.

Singh has found that these abilities tend to be more innate to women. She suspects that, "Maybe we get it more from being a parent." She finds that when women are at the table, able to effectively use these tools, successful negotiation is possible in even very contentious environments.

Her advice for aspiring leaders in public service is to discover and cultivate their unique skills that could be valuable to a country, nation, or state. "To me, it is extremely important to know the value that you bring," concludes Singh. She personally discovered that she's good at working within organizations, asking the hard questions, and helping forge consensus and coalitions. She asks her team:

- What have you tried?
- What would you be willing to try?
- What's the level of risk that you're willing to move forward with to see some level of success?

These questions lead to very different answers in every organization and country, so understanding core values is fundamental. While it is possible to read books and studies in preparation, experiencing consensus-building on the ground and engaging with people provides invaluable hands-on experience. According to Singh, diplomacy requires more than one-size-fits-all solutions and expectations. To reach effective consensus, a diplomat must understand the group, the organization, the nation, state, or whoever it is that they're working with.

Singh says that this philosophy applies to individuals in the same way it does to groups. As a diverse leader, she was asked to lead a few diversity and inclusion initiatives, which she turned down. Her thought was, "Why? Because I'm a woman? Because I'm a minority?" With diversity and inclusion, organizations often aim to have someone "diverse" leading it. But this "sends the wrong message," according to Singh. "Why not get someone who is not diverse to take it on?" she wonders. The response she usually gets is that because "they're not diverse, they don't understand the issues." But for Singh, that is the point—they need to start understanding the issues.

Non-diverse leaders need to learn what the issues are, and they can only do that if they're willing to step into these roles. Singh suggests, "Leadership should be more transparent and open when working through difficult issues of diversity and inclusion." Asking leaders to work on issues they don't understand creates opportunities for learning and change.

Swedish Ambassador Karin Olofsdotter raised a similar notion. For example, her country's Ambassador for gender issues was a man. It's "much better when a man comes and talks to other men," according to Olofsdotter.

This may seem counterintuitive to the belief that women should lead the work on gender issues or that a diverse person should lead to work on diversity issues. However, educating and changing the system may require people within the same system communicating and creating opportunities. Tamara Cofman Wittes, a senior fellow at the Center for Middle East Policy at Brookings,[49] said, "If you want innovation, if you want creativity, if you want effective problem-solving, you need diversity around the table." To bring together a group of people or a team, you need to create a coalition. Within that coalition, people can then begin to build consensus to address an issue or problem. New Zealand's Prime Minister Jacinda Ardern, for instance, made the headlines when she persuaded the male majority of a Pacific forum to build a consensus and take action on climate change.[50]

Who is around that table matters. Who builds the coalition *matters.* Women are crucial in creating impactful problem solving; whether using innate listening skills like Singh or bringing people to the table like Szemerkényi, these qualities and skillsets are how consensus is built.

---

49 Hannah Allam, "Women in National Security Push to Move Beyond 'The First' and 'The Only,'" *NPR*, July 6, 2019.
50 Eleanor Ainge Roy, "'Charismatic' New Zealand PM Jacinda Ardern named Pacific person of the year," *The Guardian,* January 6, 2020.

CHAPTER 7

EMBRACE YOUR UNIQUE VOICE

———

"It took me quite a long time to develop a voice, and now that I have it, I am not going to be silent."

—MADELEINE ALBRIGHT

FIRST WOMAN U.S. SECRETARY OF STATE

Of the questions I asked in interviews with woman foreign policy players, my favorite was the final one in which I asked each person to share a piece of wisdom. This question built my personal treasure trove of candid tips and deep-rooted knowledge from women spanning the globe. They could answer the question with the idea that this information could help rising women leaders in diplomacy and the foreign service, or simply reflect on their own impact and share their wisdom. A recurring theme began to form. To my surprise, the advice was *not* to stand up and be counted, refuse "no" as an answer, or find someone to look up to. On the contrary, the advice was to find one's own identity and embrace one's unique voice. To make an impact on the outside world, women need to be introspective.

The Honorable Mary Beth Long, introduced in Chapter 2, eloquently touches on this theme. Her pivotal piece of advice actually comes from a male colleague and mentor, and the advice changed everything for her. Early in her career, a very senior intelligence officer and her supervisor became her friend and mentor. Informed by a machismo background, he told her, "You need to know two things. You need to know that regardless of what you do in life, Mary Beth, just like every man, when people see you walk into a room, music plays in their heads. When Arnold Schwarzenegger walks in the room, it's very different music than when Danny DeVito walks into the room. When a man walks in the room like Arnold Schwarzenegger or Danny DeVito, and then *you* walk in the room, the music changes."

He shared that there are expectations and things they are thinking—solely on the account that she is a woman. He told her directly, "Don't be afraid of it—embrace it. Use it." His lesson for Long was to find the music she was going to make and make it work for her. He also warned her to not try to be somebody else's music—and as a woman, to not try to be a guy's music. The diplomatic world is male dominated, not only in the U.S. but worldwide. He shared, "It's different music when women walk in the room. And you need to write your score."

Long says she began using her music as a CIA operative undercover at the State Department in Latin America. She would walk into a room and introduce herself to particular contacts and get their business cards. The next day, she would follow up and ask them to lunch or meet. They always said yes. Her colleagues asked, "How did you get that meeting?" She embraced her music, her personal symphony, her unique voice. She used it confidently and let it play. The music allowed her to create connections other colleagues couldn't.

Her mentor's second lesson was to never work for somebody just to get ahead or because you think it will be great for women or your career. "Work for somebody who you like [and] respect, and you'll learn something from them." As a result, Long has turned down promotion opportunities because she felt it was checking a gender box or quota. She also learned that while it's tempting to work under a superstar, they might not always help pull you up in the wake of their own success.

These lessons apply to both genders. Long shared that following this advice has always served her well, because she ended up doing what she enjoyed and challenged her, and her work product reflected it. Finding and following one's music is now advice I share with anyone who will listen.

* * *

The theme spanned continents. In a meeting with a high-ranking diplomat from an African Muslim majority country, she shares that women there are also embracing their unique voices. She's agreed to speak with me under anonymity. Thus, I have taken out key identifiers to share the overall message, because the lessons are powerful. For the purposes of this book, I will refer to her as The Diplomat.

In the '60s and '70s, at a time of very few women ambassadors across the world, her country sent women ambassadors to Europe. "We've always had women take on these public roles," she shares.

Fast forwarding to current times, she says, "There has been a big push for women's rights." The Diplomat has seen her country pass reforms to gradually open up society in a sustainable manner. It's been driven internally rather than imposed by external pressure.

While she was studying abroad, she tells me, the leadership in her country changed. "I want to be part of that change," she told herself. She wondered whether she should go back to her home country to do so. The question arose, "Is it better to be outside the system or inside the system?" She ultimately decided to work in her country. For The Diplomat, it became about the small battles—the incremental change—rather than shouting about the big battles from the outside. She equates it to percentages—that 60 percent of her decision was her desire to be part of what was going on in her country, and the other 40 percent was wanting to do something that personally interested her: diplomacy.

The Diplomat graciously gives me a tour of her country's exquisite Embassy in Washington. Originally, she'd planned only to talk to me about the book overall. However, our discussion turns into a two-hour dialogue in which she quietly shares her perspective about finding her unique voice as a diplomat from Africa representing a Muslim majority country.

For our interview, The Diplomat wears a light blue shirt with simple earrings adorning her face. She speaks softly with sincerity and well-chosen words. Her calm eyes can put anyone at ease.

She and her colleagues arrived to Washington when politics were in flux. Personally, I always feel like politics in this city are in flux. That seems to be the only constant. On a professional level, she says it was "very exciting." On a personal level, though, she says she questioned herself: "This is a very important time and everybody's doubting that I can do this." The extra pressure to prove the doubters wrong was palpable. Her naysayers said a person serving in a high-ranking position in Washington needed to be at least fifty years old. She thought, "Come on?! Fifty years old? The prime minister of Canada is younger than that."

In The Diplomat's region, below the age of fifty is seen as young. Her battle began immediately, she tells me. Half of the battle was convincing her own people of her ability, and the other half was convincing the Washington elite. Most diplomats will tell you that the majority of their job depends on who the Ambassador is and how much leverage they have—if they can move things and fight for initiatives. In her case, she finds it fascinating to work for an Ambassador who has leverage in and out of the country.

The Diplomat has worked under women ambassadors in two postings so far. The U.S. is a strategic partner to many countries, and she has noticed that increasingly more strategic postings are placing women in leadership. For instance, Spain is an important partner to many African nations because of the numerous joint issues surrounding security, illegal migration, drug trafficking, arms smuggling, and economic partnership. Its proximity to Africa is vital for the region's foreign policy. Spain is a doorway connecting Europe and the African continent. She notes, "The fact that women are posted there is a significant shift."

She has seen firsthand the prominence of women ambassadors in mostly Scandinavian countries where feminist foreign policy is the norm. She says that having women appointed to strategic countries is a clear sign that women in leadership are important to the future of Africa.

When I ask her about the priorities of her country, The Diplomat shares that many people in the region are facing heated conflicts in need of resolutions. In discussions about defending issues on the international stage with colleagues, she sees her unique voice as a woman come through. Talking points tend to focus extensively on the strategic importance of the territory, the security level, the economics of the situation, and how it all plays out geopolitically—basically, the historical, political, and legal arguments. However, The Diplomat thinks about the "families who have been separated, the people who have been in exile, [and] the divided communities." She's found that most people consider any given issue solely in terms of foreign policy and forget to give voice to the people living it.

She says, "The human stories are the most powerful ones, especially when we speak with people who don't live this day in and day out as we do." While outside countries and diplomats may not know about another country's territory issue, for instance, the issue of sovereign territory is very important to those within that country.

Through her lens, The Diplomat believes that the human angle is most important in driving the narrative. To this end, she believes women are the solution. "Bring the women who are mothers and sisters, let them speak at the UN," she says confidently. She doesn't want to use the women merely for optics, but rather to provide them a platform for sharing their stories on the ground. The viewpoint of daily life from a family perspective can help move the process forward.

Embracing her unique voice in the foreign service is something The Diplomat continues to work on. In the back of her mind, she has asked herself, "Do I deserve this role? Am I competent enough? Does having a woman in the role simply look nice or am I here because there is belief in my skills with genuine respect?" Other questions pertain to her appearance to others— "How feminine should I be? How am I going to be perceived? How am I dressed? Should I wear makeup? Is it enough or too much? What if I wear no makeup at all?"

I must confess that many of the same questions have floated through my mind at different times throughout my career. Not focusing on how one is perceived by others is a constant mental battle. Private conversations with women colleagues from other Muslim majority countries reveal that the same questions exist in the back of their minds as well.

The Diplomat, however, fights back. She advises other women to not focus too much on image, but instead on "making a connection beyond the image," and investing in relationships. Diplomacy is a field in which friendships and relationships create the trust needed to have a professional edge. As she puts it, "Everybody's competing for something," whether it's information, access, or the attention of decision makers and stakeholders. What sets a person apart is the ability to establish human connections, and this skill can make all the difference in a career. Whether with people on your team or outside your country, the ultimate goal is to get people to open up.

While meeting with non-African countries, The Diplomat is constantly congratulated. "Oh wow," they say, "You're a woman, how progressive for your region!" She adds, "Even when you're not thinking about being a woman, they remind you. There are always reminders."

She awaits the day when she doesn't have to think about it—when the image of her is just that of a diplomat with a job to do. Along with her women African colleagues, The Diplomat feels that when they sit down in a meeting people see them as indicators of progress. "I hope that in the future, when people see somebody from the Middle East, Africa, or a Muslim majority country they just think, 'Oh, that's a diplomat from that country.' That's all," she says.

From candid feedback with colleagues, The Diplomat has heard that having women in leadership creates less competitiveness between the teams. Some argue competition is a good thing, but she believes that competitiveness is not always good for diplomacy. While competition may fuel ambition in other sectors, with diplomacy too much competition can create roadblocks. "You have to get along with people," she shared. That's the ultimate goal. You need to be able to be friends or allies to have a trusted relationship to exchange sensitive information and work together. The

Diplomat argues that competition and confrontation are not the same as diplomacy. "It's about working together rather than working against each other," she concluded.

Getting to a position of confidence and comfort—where you're solely focusing on getting the job done rather than what a person thinks of you—is where the magic happens.

* * *

Another woman who embraced her unique voice early in her career was Ljubica Z. Acevska from Macedonia. While Macedonia declared independence from Yugoslavia in 1991, it has an ancient history in the Balkan Peninsula. The country officially changed its name to North Macedonia in 2019 to end a bitter name dispute with Greece. For the purpose of this story, I will refer to the country as Macedonia, as Acevska's diplomatic journey took place prior to the name change. I've learned about this country through my work with the United Macedonian Diaspora, a non-government organization (NGO) addressing the interests and needs of Macedonians living outside of their homeland. The President, Metodija Koloski, warmly known as Meto, introduced me to former Ambassador Ljubica Z. Acevska.

I meet Acevska in a crowded Georgetown coffee spot where we had to search for a place to sit. After finding two seats close enough for the conversation, I notice her signature color, purple. Her purse, scarf, and shirt were purple. Even her business card was purple. When looking at photos and videos of her, I found her highlighted with . . . you guessed it, purple! What does the color purple mean? It some cultures it denotes royalty; in others, it signifies creativity and independence. With purple accents surrounding her, Acevska tells me about Macedonia establishing diplomatic relations with the U.S. and her role as Macedonia's first Ambassador. She has a lively smile, a spirited laugh, and sits with one hand on her hip with her legs crossed as she leans in to tell me her story.

Acevska was born in Capari, Macedonia, in 1957. Coming from a small village, she wasn't thrilled about emigrating to the U.S. at the age of nine. "Culturally it was very different," she remembers. Her family moved to Mansfield, Ohio, where her grandfather had previously settled and opened a restaurant in town. Her great-grandfather came to the U.S. in 1917 and her grandfather followed around 1939. She learned English in school and spoke Macedonian at home. "My parents made the biggest impact on me. They taught me the value of resilience," she tells me.

Acevska attended The Ohio State University for undergraduate and postgraduate degrees in international studies. At the university, she observed people "from all walks of life." Being open-minded and adept at meeting new people were tools she used throughout her life.

She eventually moved to Washington and became a consultant for an international trade and economic development firm. Acevska made a close woman friend who helped introduce her to the social scene. Acevska soon dove into the "Washington bubble" and discovered how to operate in the political, cultural, and social spheres. She visited Macedonia on multiple occasions, staying closely tied to her ancestral home. In the back of her mind, she thought, "[While] I'm here in Washington, I can do something to improve the relationship between the U.S. and Macedonia."

Around 1990, she looked for ways to bring investments to Macedonia. In Washington, she met with the Economic Officer from the Yugoslav representation and visiting Macedonian officials. As Yugoslavia broke up, she recommended Macedonia establish a Washington office. The officials told her to write a proposal, and they would share it with the new Macedonian President Kiro Gligorov. She never wrote it.

In 1991, Acevska traveled to Macedonia and voted in the referendum declaring Macedonia's independence. She reached out to one of the officials and asked if he had time to meet. He replied, "Sure, and how about I set up a meeting for you with the President?"

A few days before the meeting, she was visiting her family and it dawned on her: "I'm going to meet the President? I'm so young. This is ridiculous." She called the official and told him it might be better to cancel the meeting. "It's already set up, you better come," he conveyed to Acevska.

Since her Macedonian language skills were on an elementary level and unpolished, Acevska had an interpreter accompany her to the meeting. In a beautiful room around a wooden rectangular table with intricate carvings, President Gligorov met with Acevska, a journalist friend of hers, and another government official. "It was surreal. Here I was, a young woman from a small village, sitting in front of the President," she recalls.

For the first half of the meeting, the interpreter translated Acevska's words. However, she didn't think the interpreter was sufficiently conveying the meaning of the dialogue. Acevska let go of her anxiety, embraced her voice, and started speaking Macedonian. Because of that meeting, Acevska and President Gligorov established a good relationship. He then scheduled multiple meetings for her with government officials.

Before she left Macedonia, she met with him again and asked, "Mr. President, is there anything I can do when I return to Washington?" He looked at her directly, "One of the things I want to do is come to the U.S. and testify before the OSCE on what is happening in the region."

She returned to the U.S. and, within seven days, she secured an invitation for President Gligorov to testify before the OSCE and the U.S. Congress. He ended up not coming, but she had proven herself and he had faith in her. From that point, she also started to believe in herself. Some Macedonian government officials didn't understand how such a young woman could be connected to the President. However, it was her achievements and courage to get things done that allowed her accessibility to Gligorov. She derived inspiration from him as he empowered her to help the country in tangible ways.

In 1992, Acevska quit her job to become Macedonia's unofficial liaison to Washington. She recalls, "I agreed to be the liaison for a short time, but the position kept getting extended as we tried to get the U.S. to officially recognize Macedonia." She was proud and humbled to help her people.

As political attention grew around Acevska's involvement in the country's international affairs, the Macedonian press published negative comments about her. In one private conversation with Gligorov, she confided, "I don't know if I want to do this, look what they're writing about me." He listened then teased, "Well, you should read what they write about me."

In looking back, Acevska recounts many rejections to meetings and doors closed. However, she gathered her strength under the assertion that anything was possible. As the representative of a small and developing country at the time, she felt that people dismissed both Macedonia and her individually. She took it personally.

If asked to attend any event, meeting, social function, or interview, Acevska participated. Her goal was to put Macedonia on the diplomatic map. At the end of most days, she felt depleted, but her ongoing purpose gave her the renewed energy she needed to continue.

One of the most important tools for success, according to Acevska, is to believe in your purpose. She says, "If you believe in what you are doing regardless of how big the obstacles are, you will persevere and continue to do the work."

The U.S. formally recognized Macedonia in 1994, and the countries established full diplomatic relations in 1995. Acevska relinquished her U.S. citizenship in 1995 and became the first Macedonian Ambassador to the U.S. The U.S. Liaison Office, led by Acevska, was upgraded as an Embassy in 1995. When I ask if she's received any official diplomatic training,

Acevska laughs and says it was more "on-the-job training." She learned from ambassadors with established diplomatic careers to gather insight.

There were around a handful of women ambassadors in Washington at the time, and Acevska was one of the few. For public events, Acevska sometimes attended with her male Embassy colleague. "They would usually think he was the Ambassador, not me," she tells me. She recalls another instance at the White House in which President Clinton invited ambassadors and their spouses for a gathering. Acevska was single at the time and in the receiving line, and the Ambassador ahead of her was around the same age and single as well. When it was time for the official photo, the White House official said, "Please come as a couple to take a photo with the President and the First Lady," without realizing they weren't together. Acevska and the other Ambassador looked at each other and responded in unison, "We're both Ambassadors."

While those moments stuck with her, she didn't dwell on them as Macedonia had much larger issues to deal with. She says, "It's better to not be angry about those things, but to continue the work that you believe in."

Acevska also sees the need for greater gender parity in foreign policy. "As I rose in a male dominated field, I saw why it's important to have more women." While she represented Macedonia in Washington, her country hosted thousands of refugees from Bosnia in 1994 and from Kosovo in 1999. She tells me about visiting refugee camps when she returned to Macedonia and seeing "Mainly women, children, and a few old men" firsthand. Macedonia needed financial support to aid the country's inhabitants, and Acevska believes that more women at the table would have helped decision makers to better understand the issue.

In recent years, the UN reported that 50 percent of the world's refugees are women and girls, but in 2014, only 4 percent of projects in UN interagency appeals were targeted at women and girls.[51] The lack of women in decision making impacts funding for the women refugee population. This is exactly Acevska's point.

Acevska served as Ambassador until 2000 in addition to representing Macedonia at the UN General Assembly. She led the establishment of bilateral relations between Macedonia and the U.S., opened the first Macedonian Embassy in Washington, oversaw Macedonia's membership in the World Bank and International Monetary Fund, and made lasting alliances that transformed the course of her country's history.

After 2000, Acevska became a public policy scholar at the distinguished Woodrow Wilson International Center for Scholars. From 2005 to 2008, she co-hosted a D.C. talk show focusing on international issues. She also served on numerous boards and was a co-founder and president of Pencils 4 Kids International, providing school supplies to children worldwide. She reflects that "Every job is hard. You may not be easily accepted, so you have to believe in [and be certain of] yourself."

---

51   "Women Refugees and Migrants," UN Women, accessed January 19, 2020.

Acevska also believes the mentality of both women and men needs to change. Women need to embrace their unique voices, and men must transform their perceptions and listen. She says, "I hear stories of women as victims. I'm not sure that's helpful because young women may only see the obstacles in pursuing certain fields. Hearing about women as heroes is more motivational." As we speak, she shares that there is a power to stories. When she meets with young people and shares her journey, it sparks inspiration and encouragement. It makes a difference.

Acevska tells young people to not be intimidated by connecting with people of power or high positions. "Don't be afraid of rejection or deterred from something you want to pursue," she concludes. Her statement impacts me.

When I began this book project, I wondered who would be open to speaking with me. My heart raced every time I clicked "send" on an email request for an interview. In my first handful of conversations, my palms were sweaty as I nervously wrote down notes. However, the more I ventured into the process with a vision that these stories needed to be shared, my purpose strengthened. With encouragement from these inspiring women, I continued. By learning from them, I too embraced my unique voice.

CHAPTER 8

EMOTIONAL INTELLIGENCE FOR ACCESS TO POPULATIONS

———

*"You must learn to be still in the midst of
activity and to be vibrantly alive in repose."*

—INDIRA GANDHI

FIRST WOMAN PRIME MINISTER OF INDIA

There are times when diplomats must ask or negotiate for things that have no precedent. In times of war, the rules go out the door. Coalitions are broken and built. The Diplomat from an African Muslim country explains that diplomacy is necessary for conflict resolution. She says that "Exchanging with colleagues and being involved in discussions about defending an issue on the international scene" is important. However, she points out that as a woman, she sees another angle. "The weakness is that countries don't focus on the human stories behind an issue," she says. Typically, there are extensive talking points about the strategic importance of an issue, the security situation, effects on an economic level, and how it is seen geopolitically. But when you start looking at and sharing the human aspect of families being divided or exiled, she says, "it gives people a voice," which is far more effective for diplomacy.

Women tend to have access to those voices far more in war-torn countries than men. As mentioned in previous chapters, women security officers often encounter fewer boundaries than men officers when engaging civilians in domestic spaces, making them uniquely capable of gathering valuable intelligence on the ground.[52] Using emotional intelligence to read a situation and entrench oneself within a population is an essential diplomatic strategy.

As the Austrian Ambassador to Switzerland and the Former Austrian Minister for European and Foreign Affairs, Ursula Plassnik is a force among a sea of men and women. While I don't have the pleasure of interviewing her in person, we are introduced over email and she generously corresponds with me. In photos and videos, her gregarious smile and square jawline are prominent as she stands tall among many foreign dignitaries, heads of state, foreign ministers, and secretaries of state. In addition to her commanding height, videos of her speaking illustrate her sincerity of purpose, strength, and power. She truly has the presence of a leader.

---

52 "Women's Participation in Peace Processes," Council on Foreign Relations, updated January 30, 2019.

In our virtual interview, Plassnik discusses historical male power structures. She believes women perceive and respond differently to the realities in play. Plassnik writes, "In the Global Village, women's voices often go unheard." She also asks a rhetorical question: Looking at roughly 50 percent of the planet's population who are women, are they adequately represented? This is a good question, especially in international affairs where societies are formed through negotiations, peace treaties, boundaries, and laws. Plassnik notes, "Changes in the way women are treated in their respective society usually serve as a reliable indicator for the direction a society takes as a whole." In other words, some might call gender equality (or lack thereof) a canary in the coalmines.

As Austria's Foreign Minister from 2004 to 2008, Plassnik traveled to numerous nations on behalf of her country. On her first trip to the Middle East, her team arranged a visit to Ramallah to meet with women from all levels of Palestinian society for an informal lunch and discussion. Plassnik candidly shares, "No man, president, prime minister or parliamentarian has ever given me as much insight into Palestinian realities as the women I met that day."

Plassnik is of the belief that a woman's lens can reveal the realities of what the fabric of society is facing. Because many basic societal issues usually begin within a home. Plassnik acknowledges the power and nuance of meeting with women to understand the complexities of culture and country. Those informal gatherings with women became a regular feature of her scheduled trips. Her advice to all men and women? "No diplomat or politician should work without in-depth knowledge of the other 50 percent."

As a foreign policy professional at the top of her field, Plassnik sees the importance of women's perspectives everywhere. "From Mali to Afghanistan and the Democratic Republic of Congo," the world needs to learn a pivotal lesson. By reading how a situation impacts women, countries can discover the "early warnings in fragile societies." On the flip side, as the "status of women improves, the society as a whole becomes more democratic, more open, [and] more liberal."

Plassnik also relates this international relations insight to the private sector, as companies with mixed-gender teams and leadership tend to perform better. The Wharton School of the University of Pennsylvania notes that, "Companies with gender-diverse management teams have been proven to consistently perform better and be more profitable than those without them."[53] There is evidence to support the value of having more women in senior leadership positions. Studies by McKinsey & Company prove that companies with more women in senior executive and board roles have advantages over those that don't.[54]

Rather than dismissing the value of diversity, nurturing it produces better results. As stated previously, Plassnik says, "Neither the private nor the public sector can afford to disregard 50 percent of its talent, energy, and experience,"

---

53 "Does Gender Diversity on Boards Really Boost Company Performance?" Wharton School of the University of Pennsylvania, May 18, 2017. http://knowledge.wharton.upenn.edu/article/will-gender-diversity-boards-really-boost-company-performance.

54 Ibid.

* * *

Diplomacy is a living history for me. In reflecting on the trailblazers who have opened doors for women in diplomacy, it is evident that while a lot of progress has been made, there is a long way to go. Women trailblazers continue to utilize interpersonal skills to forge greater access to populations. In our nation's capital, I have worked with and befriended these diplomats from various countries.

One of my connections with the utmost emotional intelligence is the Deputy Chief of Mission Lara Romano at the Croatian Embassy in Washington. She is a "get-things-done" leader in the field of diplomacy. We previously co-hosted a dinner at the Croatian Ambassador's residence with the organization I work for. No detail was left out—Romano orchestrated the flow of the dinner and evening and was an expert maestro throughout the conversation.

Romano exudes a dashing determination when she walks into a room. Her perfectly shaped dark eyebrows and high cheekbones emphasize her eyes as she makes direct eye contact during conversations. Her poise and the intensity of her gaze encourages people to make a connection.

Romano has always been curious about her family's Jewish background from Sarajevo. When she was growing up, her father shared that her great grandfather was the last Rabbi of Yugoslavia—an honor in the historic community. To continue tracing her lineage and understanding her family's history, Romano decided to move to Israel. She learned Hebrew while living and working on a communal farm called a Kibbutz. Eventually she attended Tel Aviv University. Since Judaism was barely a part of her upbringing, learning and understanding the culture took effort and persistence. Having obtained a degree in art history and theater, Romano shares that a career in foreign affairs and diplomacy was far from her mind.

Instead, she envisioned a career as a Renaissance art researcher and theatre critic. Romano applied for M.A. program at Oxford and was accepted. She tried to get funding to attend but never received a scholarship. Disappointed, she left Israel and moved back to Croatia. She recalls being fresh out of university with a diploma in hand, wondering what to do next. She decided to seek her father's advice.

He told her, "Listen, I saw this ad at the Croatian paper. They're looking for people who speak both Hebrew and Croatian to work for the Croatian Foreign Ministry. You should send in your CV and apply for the position!" Without a background in political science or diplomacy, she reluctantly submitted her application. Croatia had recently established diplomatic relations with Israel, and was seeking young graduates who spoke Hebrew upon opening its first Embassy in Tel Aviv. Romano was three months out from graduation when she got her first job with the Croatian Embassy. Her first thought was, "I have absolutely no idea what I'm going to be doing."

Romano began her diplomatic career as a local staff member and enjoyed it, so she worked her way up to becoming a career diplomat. With more than twenty years in diplomacy and many women superiors, Romano has discovered the impact of diverse voices in negotiations and forging peace.

One of her most formative experiences was Romano's field assignment with the International Security Assistance Force (ISAF), a NATO-led security mission in Afghanistan. She served in a dual-hatted role as political advisor to a NATO Senior Civilian Representative and as a coordinator for Croatian bilateral development projects with Afghan women and children. Romano was the first Croatian woman diplomat to serve in Afghanistan.

This posting gave her a unique opportunity to see the UN resolutions she negotiated for Croatia—adopted in New York and Geneva—translated into real life. She saw firsthand how important it was to have women participate in negotiations and implementation of policy, as the women in Afghanistan play an important role. Romano shares the sentiment that "You cannot negotiate with 50 percent of the population being left out." Women are frequently victims of war, and having women support them through NATO had "a strong psychological impact" for the Afghan women.

Romano elaborates, "As part of the Western community, as a woman diplomat serving in Afghanistan, being there at the decision-making table, and participating in the stabilization efforts for the country, [civilians] see you as an example of how they can rise and be part of that same process. So, it's leading by example."

In her role as NATO political advisor, Romano lived on a compound predominantly surrounded by military personnel and was tasked with activities supporting the 2014 provincial and presidential elections, monitoring the election on the ground, and participating in daily NATO headquarter briefings for the military. Romano also made daily visits outside of the compound to local women and children involved in ongoing Croatian bilateral projects. It was a huge responsibility, but also a privilege. As a civilian and a woman diplomat, she was often welcomed into places where the military and men were excluded. Her inside perspective added nuance to on-the-ground deliberations. She says she became part of the team that was the "eyes and ears within the Afghan community" for NATO.

Without a large budget for bigger projects like Germany or Sweden, Croatia focused on smaller community investments under the slogan "Small Projects—Significant Effects." At the time, the woman Croatian Foreign Minister decided the humanitarian projects should center on Afghan women and children, specifically on women in entrepreneurship. Those investments have been the most fruitful by using a relatively small amount of funding; thus, local women were able to improve their life conditions while supporting the local community.

Statistics prove that when women work, they invest 90 percent of their income back into their families, compared to 35 percent among men.[55] By being on the ground as a woman Croatian diplomat, Romano improved access to that contingent of the population by gaining their trust. As a result, she was invited into Afghan homes and private spaces to take part in women's discussions.

---

55 "Empowering Girls & Women," Clinton Global Initiative, accessed January 25, 2020.

In the process of understanding the culture, Romano discovered that weddings were one of the most important celebrations for Afghans. However, since the celebration was separated between men and women, most women did not have their wedding celebrations photographed, as they were uncomfortable having men photograph or record them. Romano helped create a photography training workshop as one of the Croatian development projects. "We taught women how to learn to use cameras and video cameras, so they could serve as photographers during those occasions. So those little things, which didn't cost that much money, made a huge difference in their lives," recalls Romano.

One project was particularly significant and close to her heart—the Croatian Government flagship project. It established a Center for Midwives to serve as an educational school for young women coming from nine northern Afghan provinces. Through education and training, the goal was to reduce child and maternal mortality. As a result of the deteriorating security situation, there wasn't a formal opening ceremony upon the project's completion. Romano hopes to return someday to see the center and the important goal it is achieving.

Due to the growing security concerns and the ever-changing situation on the ground, Croatia eventually recalled its diplomats from the NATO mission in Afghanistan. Romano regretted the decision because it was an important part of diplomatic work and invaluable field experience. She tells me how traveling in the field and working directly with Afghans without weapons or media were some of the most challenging and rewarding parts of the mission. "We must remember that sometimes it takes risk to do little things that create impact and value," noted Romano.

Through the difficulties she has encountered, Romano has learned that "Those situations made me the person and the diplomat I am today." She doesn't underestimate the process of growing, evolving, and learning, and tells others, "Don't get discouraged, don't give up." She admits she was tempted many times to yield throughout different diplomatic postings whenever she encountered the infamous wall or ceiling. Only now—when she hears a negative comment or is put in a difficult situation—will Romano take a step back for introspection and breathe. She then continues on her path wiser, stronger, and more determined, using the lessons learned to her advantage.

Overall, Romano believes in the inclusivity of both women and men as an effective problem-solving strategy. She has found that a mixture of military, diplomatic, and civilian components is valuable for peace solutions. When women are part of teams and able to provide their professional expertise and emotional intelligence, they have the advantage of access. They can facilitate information sharing, build confidence and trust, and change the situation on a significant scale. The Council on Foreign Relations affirms that when women and civil society groups participate in peace processes and negotiations, agreements are 35 percent more likely to last fifteen years.[56]

---

56 "Women's Participation in Peace Processes," Council on Foreign Relations, updated January 30, 2019.

The Organization for Security and Co-operation in Europe (OSCE) toolkit for the "Inclusion of Women and Effective Peace Processes" supports these findings. For example, the OSCE found that establishing a trust-based relationship with advisors is essential. From research, respondents noted that women advisors tended to establish good relationships with "conflict-affected communities," especially with local women and civil society. It also found that "women were seen as able to open the hearts and minds of people, including detainees and prisoners."[57]

* * *

An essential part of diplomacy is the ability to open the hearts and minds of local populations. Emotional intelligence is a skill Ambassador Martha Bárcena brings to her job every day. Bárcena is the first woman Mexican Ambassador to be posted in Washington. After entering the Mexican Embassy off Pennsylvania Avenue, I make my way through the security check, and the friendly Embassy staff escort me upstairs to meet the Ambassador. The red, green, and white flag is prominently on display in the waiting room, anchored with a red couch and armchairs. Mexican art hangs on the walls and a book about avocados sits on a coffee table. Spanish quietly floats through the air as the Embassy staff walk the hallways.

Ambassador Bárcena arrives from another meeting, and the staff graciously walk me to her office, carrying a glass of

---

57   Leena Avonius, Meeri-Maria Jaarva, Ulrike Schmidt, and Talia Wohl, "Inclusion of Women and Effective Peace Processes: A Toolkit," Organization for Security and Co-operation in Europe (OSCE), accessed January 12, 2020.

water for me on a silver tray. White walls and carpet adorn the large space. A grand, ornate wooden desk is centered in the Ambassador's office. Given the size and solid foundation, the thought passes through my mind that five people could easily dance on top of it. We sit at the opposite side of the room on plush green and white striped sofa chairs near an elaborate wood bookcase with antique books. Bárcena is a career diplomat with a kind smile and warm brown eyes. Pearl earrings and a matching necklace frame her face, and she wears a scarf folded delicately on top of her gray-blue sweater. Her disposition is serious but welcoming.

Born in Veracruz, Mexico, Bárcena joined the Mexican Foreign Service in 1979. She served as Consul to Barcelona from 1989 to 1990; Ambassador to Denmark, Norway, and Iceland from 2004 to 2013; Ambassador to Turkey, Georgia, Azerbaijan, Kazakhstan and Turkmenistan from 2013 to 2017; and Permanent Representative of Mexico to the United Nations Agencies in Rome from 2017 to 2018. Representing Mexico literally took Bárcena around the world.

Her educational background is in Communication Sciences and Philosophy, with a master's degree in International Studies from the Diplomatic School in Spain and another master's degree in Political Philosophy from Universidad Iberoamericana. In addition to Spanish, Bárcena speaks English, French, and Italian with a working knowledge of German, Danish, and Chinese.

I continue to be highly impressed that most diplomats speak multiple languages. I studied Spanish in middle school, high school, and college, yet I can only speak in the present tense.

As far as my Spanish skills are concerned, nothing ever happened in the past and it's not possible to look to the future— all that we have is the present. In case it isn't obvious, the entire interview with Bárcena is conducted in English.

Bárcena's glasses perch on top of her head as she explains, "In diplomacy, especially with bilateral relations, we have the challenge [of] explain[ing] what the other person means." Finding areas of common interest and understanding helps diplomats to solve problems with emotional intelligence.

Bárcena learned this lesson as a young diplomat. While serving in the consular service in San Diego, she traveled to the border of the U.S. and Mexico for an official visit to a detention center. She was the only woman among her colleagues.

During the visit, a young woman approached her and discreetly shared her experience of being "mistreated by the border patrol with threats and abuse." The young woman was cautious about telling the men who were in charge of protecting Mexicans at the detention center because she didn't think men could be trusted. Under her capacity as a diplomat, Bárcena had access to vulnerable populations and this woman's trust. From that experience, Bárcena understood that "having women for very specific tasks regarding consular services is important." In delicate situations, women tend to confide or trust in other women.

Later in her career and work with the UN, Bárcena saw firsthand how "women representing UN agencies can be helpful, especially with connecting to other women in refugee situations or with those suffering from a disaster." In her role with the World Food Program, she saw how women divulged more to one another than to men when sharing certain experiences. "Women can inspire more trust and ask the right questions which aid in evaluating the gender perspective and helps with women empowerment," Bárcena tells me. She also notes "that the most successful teams have a mix of women and men working together with different sensibilities for the same problem within the same approach."

Throughout our conversation, Bárcena shares that both women and men can be effective negotiators. However, women seem to seek out the intersection of interests instead of being obsessed with solely promoting issue positions. Finding the intersection of interests in negotiation can help lead to resolutions.

During her post as Ambassador to Turkey around 2015, Bárcena remembered "difficult times" such as bombings in Ankara. As the Syrian Civil War gained momentum, she interacted with Syrian refugees in the Turkish refugee camps. She recalls being deeply moved by "how resilient people are, especially in difficult conditions." In speaking to Syrian refugees or Mexicans in detention centers, Bárcena found a connecting thread: the strength of families. The desire to keep their families and children together served as the primary source of resilience for refugees in vulnerable situations.

Bárcena admits that this was a difficult part of her job, describing herself as "very emotional." She has heard the following many times: "Ambassador or Consul, I cannot stay here for two weeks to be a material witness because I'm the one supporting my family, and how can I leave since I am the one who needs to work and send money?"

While Bárcena remembers taking part in crafting the convention of human rights and migrant workers, negotiating the tariff and trade situation, and aiding in labor reform for Mexico, she considers all those actions as "part of the job." However, she adds, "I think the most moving moments always have to do with the personal experiences of other people." She says that seeing how your job has "helped someone in a very vulnerable condition or when you interact with someone who has changed the world like an artist or musician," you understand how the work of diplomacy changes perspectives unlike any other occupation.

To foreign service officers, Bárcena recommends taking time to understand the location when posted to a new country. "Between the hours that you spend in the office, spend part of your time simply going around, seeing people, talking to people, and understanding the culture in which you have just landed," she shared. Bárcena also suggests reading poetry, novels, and literature from the country, claiming that, "Reading allows you to glimpse the soul of the country."

In reflecting on her foreign service career, Bárcena recognizes that women are still working their way to gaining more seats at the table. Of her own leadership, she says, "I am the first woman Ambassador to the U.S. from Mexico. I broke the glass ceiling, but we still have a long way to go." In photographs from the negotiations on the issue of the threat of tariffs and migration in June 2019, you can see only two women at the table, the Secretary of Economy and Bárcena. In September, the photographs changed and Bárcena was the only woman at the table.

Bárcena calls for "more women at defense ministries and national security councils." She also applauds that in Mexico, there is now a woman interior minister for the first time. In spite of this, Bárcena says, the lack of gender equality around the table persists. She is also concerned about increased political polarization in countries. She hopes that "public diplomacy doesn't contribute to the terrible polarization that we're seeing in societies," but rather that it contributes to the "smoothing of polarization inside countries and between countries."

The Mexican and U.S. border was another topic of our discussion. In Bárcena's opinion, how the border has been portrayed in recent years is "totally wrong and biased." The image that "the border is equal to crime and lawlessness has a political intention." She says firmly, "There are problems, yes, but the border is much more than that."

"We have a lot of problems that we cannot deny such as sanitation, organized crime, and drug trafficking, but the border also offers a lot of opportunities," explains Bárcena. She says if a country could be made out of the border including the six Mexican states and four U.S. states such as California, Texas, New Mexico, Arizona, Baja, Sonora, Chihuahua, Coahuila, Nuevo Leon, and Tamaulipas, that country of ten states would be the third-largest economy in the world. While I don't have exact data to support this notion, the idea is fascinating.

Bárcena describes the contributions of migrants in the United States—a country purportedly based on the ideals of immigration. "It is very painful to listen to all the rhetoric that tries to equate immigrants to criminals. It's a political manipulation that is unacceptable," Bárcena cautions. While there are criminals among immigrants, there are also criminals among permanent populations. Criminals are "not what unites America and Mexico." She counters that we must recognize how "geography, history, cultural ties, and family will always bind us together."

Bárcena emphasizes the marital nature of the relationship between the United States and Mexico: "We are in a marriage where we can't divorce, so it better be a happy marriage, not a marriage that is fighting the whole time." Like any marriage, maintaining peace in this relationship takes work. Though representing her country is her job, Bárcena sees this work as an honor. She describes her philosophy as, "Take yourself seriously in your job, but don't become obsessed."

Bárcena still feels enormous pride during the Mexican Independence Day by representing and celebrating Mexico with the Mexican diaspora in whatever country she is posted. The special ceremony features a call-and-response portion with the audience and then the national anthem plays. "I've been doing it for the last sixteen years and every time, I have a lump in my throat."

For Bárcena, remembering the connection to her home country is crucial. She is of the belief that in order to help others, a diplomat must remember the country they represent and why they are there in the first place.

Leaders like Plassnik, Romano, and Bárcena illustrate the crucial need for emotional intelligence in diplomacy, especially when working with vulnerable populations. These leaders also recognize the importance of their gender in gaining access to groups and spaces in a fundamentally different manner than their male colleagues. Both genders offer unique strengths that enable better problem-solving and cooperation around the table.

PART 3

STABILITY: DIVERSITY BUILDS PEACE

CHAPTER 9

INCLUSIVENESS FOR SOLUTIONS

———

"I hate to say there are female and male ways of dealing with power because I think each of us has a male and a female part. But based on my own experience, women will tend to be inclusive, to reach out more, to care a little more."

—CHRISTINE LAGARDE

FIRST WOMAN CHAIR AND MANAGING DIRECTOR

OF THE INTERNATIONAL MONETARY FUND

In the progress of this book, I encounter many examples of how women in leadership create space for inclusiveness. The same theme arises in my conversation with Finnish Ambassador Kirsti Kauppi. We meet in her modern office with no drapes, just glass windows looking out on the greenery of the Embassy grounds in Washington. She shares that in addition to the valuable input women have to offer, their mere presence at the table—whether two or three or more to "represent issues related to peace or development"—can trigger certain discussions.

According to Kauppi, the question that is usually missed in the absence of women at the table is, how does X, Y, or Z impact women or children? This aspect is typically "dismissed if no women are around."

Data from 1992 to 2018 shows that women represented 3 percent of mediators, 13 percent of negotiators, and 4 percent of witnesses and signatories in all major peace processes.[58] The lack of women present for these initiatives is deafening. If women help build inclusiveness for society, they need to be involved in policy formation.

A UN Security Council report from 2018 states, "Gender-sensitive language in peace agreements is critical to setting a foundation for gender inclusion during the peacebuilding phase."[59] Evidence also shows that when women are included in peace process initiatives, there is a 20 percent increase in the probability of an agreement lasting two years, and a 35 percent increase of it lasting for 15 years.[60]

---

58 "Women's Participation in Peace Processes," Council on Foreign Relations, updated January 30, 2019.

59 "Report of the Secretary-General on Women, Peace and Security," UN Security Council, October 9, 2019. S/2019/800, 2019: 6.

60 Oisika Chakrabarti and Sharon Grobeisen, "Media advisory: UN Women Highlights the Voices of Women Building Sustainable Peace and Mobilizing for Justice and Equality," UN Women, October 23, 2017.

In her dark rimmed-glasses, Kauppi noted that women bring a "respectful approach" to the table and "try to involve everybody." She firmly believes both women and men are needed at the table and both genders equally contribute to peace-building solutions.

Throughout my conversation with Kauppi, she says women tend to have more self-doubt— something she thinks is changing in upcoming generations. That said, she believes there is a "silver lining." This inherent self-doubt encourages women to "test their decisions and assumptions" and invite probing, collaboration, and different points of view. By making the "threshold lower to disagree," women utilize inclusiveness to build long-lasting solutions. You'll hear more in the next chapter about Ambassador Kauppi and how the Finnish government is paving the way for gender equality around the table.

* * *

Sociopolitical stability is often a goal of diplomacy. Being inclusive and open-minded to ideas around the table can help to more efficiently reach goals and achieve stability in a region. Albanian Ambassador to the U.S. Floreta Faber uses this approach frequently.

I recall meeting her multiple times through my work. She is always poised and focused. Tan bricks lined the exterior of the Embassy where I've come to meet her. I've passed by the building many times without realizing what was inside. It's a former historic home with high ceilings and detailed woodwork. I climb the elegant staircase that opens up to the grand living space with multiple rooms.

We sit for the interview behind two large wooden sliding doors, in white cream chairs with bronze embellishments surrounding a long, elegant table. Faber wears a long royal blue jacket that exemplifies her strong and confident presence. Like most ambassadors, her schedule is quite busy. She tries to say yes to as many events as possible, as representing her country is not just a job to her, but rather a personal priority and honor. With a small team, she is the face of Albania in America.

Born in Shkoder, Albania, on March 19, 1968, Faber was the youngest of three daughters. Her sisters learned to speak French while she went to English classes. Everyone in her family was an educator. She believes her parents and her sisters played a pivotal role in her life, helping her become who she is today.

Faber discusses the history of gender in Albania. She says, "We came from a history of what we called a socialist country and from the outside they called a communist country. Around the '60s, some of the decisions made in the government were completely wrong, while others played a positive role in society. One of the positive ones, in my perspective, was that men and women [were granted] the same rights. The pay was generally equal as well, but decision making has been and is still male-dominated." For all of its faults, Soviet-style political systems did entail a degree of gender equity.

Faber graduated in 1990 from Tirana University in Albania with a focus on economics. She then studied international marketing and strategy for her master's degree at the Norwegian School of Management in Oslo. She was briefly an exchange student at the Washington State University, and she completed her graduate degree in marketing and operational management in Albania.

After the drastic fall of communism in 1991, Albania reestablished diplomatic relations with the U.S. The country was essentially "starting from scratch." Faber remembers Albania didn't have private property and had zero private businesses. From 1990 until 1993, she gained professional experience working for the Chamber of Commerce, a Regional Business Agency, and a public import-export company. From 1995 to 2000, Faber worked for Deloitte & Touche in Albania and the Czech Republic. The American Chamber of Commerce officially opened in Albania in 2000, and Faber served as its Executive Director. She tells me that she worked in a "diplomatic sense," as she had to negotiate with the government, private sector, and international community leaders all while keeping a balance of impartiality and transparency.

In 2013, the new government began to ask Albanian leaders from different fields to assume government offices. Faber recalled the appointed Minister of Culture had a literature background as a publisher and was a translator. Faber's work with the American Chamber of Commerce allowed her to communicate regularly with government officials, and they wanted her to bring a different perspective to Washington as the Ambassador.

Since her background was not in politics and she wasn't in the Foreign Ministry, the change was difficult for her family. She tells me that her husband had to take leave from being a cardiovascular surgeon, and her two children were reluctant to say goodbye to their friends.

Faber continues, "If you are already in the field of diplomacy, you're raised with the idea that you go from one place to another, but for us, it was really out of the blue." Faber and her husband discussed the posting and the possible impact on their family. He supported her: "You have a one-time opportunity, let's try it." However, she understood that this was a difficult decision and a major sacrifice for him to move away from his profession.

Faber presented her credentials as Ambassador of Albania to the United States on May 18, 2015. She also represents her country's interests in Mexico, the Dominican Republic, and Panama. As the first woman in the role, she embarked on what she calls a "listening tour." Faber contacted almost all of Albania's previous ambassadors who had been posted to Washington. She wanted to hear about their experiences and ideas of what worked and what didn't.

When she arrived, she looked at the opportunity differently than her predecessors. She says, "I wanted to open the Embassy to the U.S. public and Albanians living in the United States." The previous ambassadors didn't see how that would make a difference in the diplomatic realm and representing Albania. Meetings with outsiders were typically held at restaurants or cafes. Generally, the Embassy was not open to the public except on the annual national day.

This became clear to Faber three days after she arrived in Washington, she tells me. She had come to the Embassy on a Saturday to get acquainted with her new role. While on the third floor, she heard a knock coming from downstairs. She went to the door and opened it.

"Is the Embassy open today?" asked the visitor.

Faber replied, "No, it's a Saturday."

"Oh, well we thought it was open today."

Faber thought to herself, "That was odd," as she walked back up to the third floor. A few minutes later, she heard another knock at the door. A similar conversation happened. She called her Embassy team and asked them what was going on. They told her it was the annual Around the World Embassy Open House—a day for the public to visit certain embassies and learn about each country and culture. Faber's colleagues shared that while most embassies opened their doors, Albania had never participated. She says she told her staff, "From now on, we're going to open the Embassy doors every year." She was determined to be as inclusive as possible and put Albania on the diplomatic map. Faber's experience in the private sector made her results-driven and achieving goals runs through her blood.

The building itself was freshly renovated from a four-year project when Faber arrived. However, it needed to be decorated and organized in order to function as a welcoming space. The diplomatic team along with Faber happened to be all women serving in the newly refurbished Embassy. During the first two years of her posting, the all-women team efficiently made changes to the Embassy with the limited resources they had. Faber and the team hand-picked items and placed them throughout the building.

While describing the situation to me, Faber looks around the elegant room from the drapes to the chairs. She taps her finger on the long table with a slight chuckle and says, "I have personally worked on everything that you see here." For her, the Embassy is a space for welcoming people on behalf of her country. Because of their small population, their power "isn't in the military or economy," she notes. Instead, the "nature of the Albanian culture, religion, tolerance, and passion for life" are things she wants people to learn about and appreciate. Welcoming people for events is similar to welcoming people into your home, according to Faber. It's the "details and compassion" that make the difference. "It has made a difference in many ways in how we present the country and ways we've been able to make contacts by opening the Embassy for meetings and events," Faber says.

Opening the Embassy to the public was part of a larger initiative. On top of the "political, diplomatic, economic, and cultural relationships," Faber emphasizes the importance of working with the Albanian diaspora. Some of the younger generations of Albanians living in the U.S. have never visited their ancestral home. Faber started a program to bring young Albanian Americans to Washington for two days to showcase Albania. They visit institutions, members of congress, and government agencies with whom Albania closely works. The goal is to include the young leaders and encourage them to think of ways to include Albania on the global stage. "In diplomacy, you have to be passionate and creative," Faber shares. This motivation propels her to excel at representing her country.

In discussing how women tend to be inclusive, Faber shares that she has found women are focused and able to shed their egos. She explains, "If I have a goal to reach related to my job,

I don't mind who I have to speak to and how many silences I have to break." It seems that as a woman diplomat, at some point while representing your country, you will find yourself in a male-dominated room, wondering if you should say something or not. But in the realm of diplomacy, if you don't speak, your country doesn't speak and will not be represented. Inclusion is not solely about including others. Being inclusive is also about proactively including yourself.

For Faber, cultivating inclusive team dynamics is imperative for success. Her business background inspired her to institute an evaluation process to improve her staff's professional experience at the Embassy. For this and all initiatives, she seats everyone around the table to share creative ideas. "You have to make everyone feel a part of it so everyone can be a part of the success," she notes. Faber makes a point to share publicly that everything they do is a "team effort."

Under her leadership, the Embassy has seen an increase in the number of visiting delegations from Albania, official government meetings with the United States, and increased visibility within the American public sphere and among the Albanian diaspora.

* * *

National Security and Communications Expert Lauren Protentis—a rising woman leader in the world of diplomacy—also espouses the tangible benefits of inclusion. Protentis and I met in my graduate program at Georgetown University. During one of our in-person residency weeks, we found out we had a mutual person in common: her husband. I went to undergraduate school with him "down south" in the state of Georgia and recalled hearing about his marriage to a "northerner from Massachusetts."

Protentis and I have attended the same weddings and football tailgates without knowing one another until graduate school. It is clear why my friend married her. Protentis is smart, strong, confident, and simultaneously exudes charm. From our first interaction in graduate school to our many personal conversations, I am continually impressed by her as a person and a leader. Together, we learned the importance of global strategic communications, and we continue to discuss how to promote gender equity in policy and diplomacy.

Protentis is a granddaughter of a Holocaust survivor and daughter of a federal agent. Service and humanitarianism run through her veins. In her own words, "I was taught at a very young age to challenge the *status quo*, and never to settle for any sort of social injustice." She has held a few roles at the U.S. Department of State—including program specialist, senior communications manager, Deputy Chief, and Director of Interagency Engagement leading external affairs, communications and strategy to develop solutions to the emerging trends in communications, disinformation, and propaganda.

In 2018, she spent a year at the Foreign and Commonwealth Office, a department of the Government of the United Kingdom, in London, leading multilateral cooperation on policy initiatives and counter-ISIS communications to confront disinformation and propaganda. With her Bostonian background, Protentis has a style exuding a classy blend of Jackie

O. with a splash of Coco Chanel. Protentis has a noticeably vivacious smile that vibrates across a room. Whether at a cocktail reception or a high-profile meeting, her disposition is magnetic.

Protentis studied Arabic prior to her time with the State Department. In 2011, she attended the Arabeya Language Institute in Cairo, Egypt. Her apartment looked over Tahrir Square. The Arab Spring was in full force and violent protests erupted. With the help of her father's federal influence, she was evacuated to Israel.

In 2012, Protentis joined the U.S. State Department. Meanwhile, across the globe, an international threat emerged. At the height of its power, ISIS boasted 100,000 fighters in arms,[61] controlled 41,000 square miles of territory in Iraq and Syria, and developed a dangerous terrorist network that could strike the heart of Europe and beyond."[62]

Protentis recalls an exchange initiative at the State Department in which she heard from a mother whose son joined a terrorist organization and died fighting near Aleppo, Syria. Protentis says, matter-of-factly, "It was no surprise that the only attendees in the room to hear the mother were women." She continues, "For me, and the other women in the room, we were there to understand the audience. Listening was the first step to do[ing] something effective."

---

61 Liz Sly, "Islamic State May Still Have 30,000 Fighters in Iraq and Syria, Even After Setbacks," *The Washington Post*, August 14, 2018.

62 Mattisan Rowan, "ISIS After the Caliphate," The Wilson Center, updated January 8, 2018.

Protentis stresses the importance of understanding an audience for effective communication. This listening exercise triggered a whole series of events for Protentis, as she started thinking that women—especially mothers—could be a tool the State Department could use to defeat ISIS. She says, "I'm always encouraging governments to think about leveraging the voices of women."

Protentis explains that the mother is the cornerstone of the family in the Muslim faith. After that meeting, Protentis went to three of her women colleagues and said, "This is our way. This is the path. We need to activate mothers globally to do two things: to dissuade potential recruits from joining ISIS, and to get their stories out to create fissures in the ISIS recruitment narrative."

In response to the national security and defense angle to fighting ISIS, many in the room proposed operations to stop the flow of foreign fighters. Her plan, on the other hand, took another route aiming for non-operational grass-roots mobilizing.

According to the National Bureau of Economic Research, "As of December 2015, approximately 30,000 fighters from at least 85 countries had joined ISIS.[63] Although the great majority of ISIS recruits come from the Middle East and the Arab world, there are also many from Western nations, including most member-states of the European Union, the United States, Canada, Australia, and New Zealand. Thousands of fighters

---

63 Les Picker, "Where Are ISIS's Foreign Fighters Coming From?," *The NBER Digest*, The National Bureau of Economic Research, June 2016.

from Russia and hundreds from Indonesia and Tajikistan have also joined. ISIS's recruitment of foreign fighters is a global phenomenon that provides the organization with the human capital needed to operate outside the Middle East."

To combat ISIS's communication strategy, Protentis recalls, "We created a grassroots mobilization effort." Mothers whose children had joined ISIS led the network to train other mothers to recognize signs of radicalization. Eventually fathers and siblings joined the network too. The idea grew from one organization to dozens then to seventy-five spanning four continents and twenty countries. Protentis reflects that "There was clearly a community demand for this type of engagement."

Protentis described it as an organic network of organizations working in communities across Europe and North Africa and eventually Asia to prevent radicalization, counter violent extremism, and fight back against terrorism. "That was my pivotal moment," she says. "It made me feel proud of women working for women to affect change."

Protentis again emphasizes the importance of inclusive relationships. "When I look at the core of women I had the chance to work with, it's always about the group. It's always about getting ahead together versus one by one. And it's an inclusive approach. We're looking out for each other's success in the long run. It's a sisterhood."

Despite these successes, Protentis reflects that she and other women colleagues were sometimes at a disadvantage because they were viewed as young, inexperienced, and female. "I continue to be challenged when walking into a room of serious people. Many of them are men, many of them are in uniforms. Many of them are two decades older than me. I think, 'Do I sit at the table or do I sit in the backbench?' I constantly feel I shouldn't be sitting at the table, [almost like] I should be sitting in the back."

Sitting at the table is a constant theme among women diplomats. Who is at the table or who is at the back of the room? Protentis says she experienced a turning point in her career when asked to brief the Counterterrorism Advisor to President Trump. Protentis remembers thinking, "I'm not the right person. I don't know enough. Even though I put this plan together, I can't do this."

Her office encouraged her to go. The morning of the briefing was a disaster—printers weren't working, locked bags for materials were misplaced, and documents were printed only minutes before she had to leave for the National Security Council. Her heart raced as she proceeded through multiple locked doors into a "situation room." It's the place where the nation's top national security issues are debated and where the President makes decisions.

The air in the room was stuffy with seriousness and men. She immediately started looking for an excuse to sit in the back row away from the table, but in order to present, she knew she had to be at the table. To combat her fear, Protentis did two things.

First, she walked around the room and individually introduced herself to everyone. She knew that introducing herself would immediately humanize the group and environment. It allowed her to engage in a manner that felt natural and less anxiety-inducing.

Second, Protentis decided to be herself. "Just being me is more effective than walking in and trying to mirror everybody else around me. My personality, as it turns out, is very disarming. I find that [it] creates the opening for dialogue and tends to put others at ease."

The meeting started and everyone introduced themselves. "It's the Ambassador from X country on the line, its X senior official on the line, and so on . . ." Protentis recalls that when it was her time to speak, her beating heart slowed and anxiety eased. The Counterterrorism Advisor walked in, sat at the table and opened the meeting books. The meeting started, and Protentis recognized that she was one of only four women at the table and on the international call. She delivered her presentation and proudly represented her office.

After her presentation, she says, the fear was completely gone. "At the end of the meeting, the Counterterrorism Advisor verbally applauded me. He told me privately, 'You did a fantastic job. I'm seeing a lot of good work coming out of your office, and I'll be sure to let your seniors know.' I left the meeting thinking, 'I can do this. I can do anything!'"

The program that Protentis helped create was an integral piece of the puzzle to combat ISIS. Defeating ISIS and confidently taking her seat at the table is only the beginning for Protentis. With her efforts to build inclusive solutions, national security and foreign policy will benefit from her voice.

The views expressed are her own and not those of the U.S. Government.

* * *

Another woman I interviewed from both the private and public sector shared how the importance of understanding a culture and its people builds a foundation of inclusiveness for diplomacy.

Former U.S. Ambassador Lisa Guillermin Gable can usually be spotted in a crowd. With her neatly coiffed hair and incandescent smile, Gable radiates in any room. Her clear voice and organized train of thought illustrate how she's been able to accomplish many roles in her life, including nonprofit CEO, political advisor, U.S. Ambassador, UN Delegate, corporate executive, and a board member to a few organizations.

To this day, she still feels that one of the secrets of her success is her willingness to understand and "engage on a very personal level within a country." Meeting people in places that are important to them creates an inclusive connection. Throughout Gable's career, she has been able to focus her strengths and weave her business acumen into diplomacy. Her time as a diplomat in Japan is merely one example of this.

President George W. Bush appointed Gable as the first woman to serve as a U.S. Ambassador to the World Fair in Japan. It was the first time the role had been filled by a woman in more than 180 years. Gable recognized that as a working mother of a young child, she engaged with her role differently than her male colleagues, many of whom were much older and had considerable experience under their belts.

Her task was to take the economically challenged World Fair model and make it a success with no federal funds. The $33.7 million operation had more than seventy employees, and Gable quickly moved to re-position U.S. involvement by focusing on business development and job creation.

She took her raw skills and go-getter attitude to develop personal relationships with top Japanese CEOs and political leaders. She sought to create direct partnerships between key economic centers in the U.S. and Nagoya, home of the Toyota Motor Corporation.

The U.S. Congress was very unhappy with previous financial obligations and spending associated with the World's Fair. She recalled the infamous tale of the White City, which is about the Chicago World's Fair. The event was a financial burden to the town. It also attracted Chicago's first documented serial killer, who killed at least twenty-seven women who came to work at the fair and cremated them in a lime pit in his basement.[64]

Put lightly, the World's Fair was seen as a challenge with huge financial overrun, and Gable was in charge of taking the completely privatized project and making it financially viable with no infrastructural support from the U.S. government. In other words, as a U.S. Ambassador with many legal technicalities related to fundraising, Gable was tasked with producing the first U.S. World's Fair operation under budget and on time.

---

64   "The Devil in the White City," *WTTW News*, Chicago PBS, accessed July 27, 2019.

The position was a major milestone for Gable that guided the rest of her career. She utilized her understanding of navigating government regulations with complex legal structures and politics to fund the event through business support and meet the needs of the government. Gable tells me that she saw firsthand "how we can use business as part of our diplomacy efforts to meet both diplomatic and other types of requirements."

In the process of leading U.S. involvement in the World's Fair, it was important for Gable to visit smaller cities in the host country of Japan and understand the national culture. She carries this diplomatic skillset with her throughout her career and travels. Gable also had her six-year-old daughter with her during the posting. As one of the few women involved in the project, and uniquely as a mother with a small child, she decided to bring her daughter with her for the experience. Her daughter drew pictures and wrote thank you notes to everyone they met, from diplomats to high-level CEOs. Gable recalls how "We would go in the offices of the CEO from some of the largest companies in the world and they had her thank you note pasted up on their desk."

During one particularly long, exhausting day, Lisa Gable found herself in a small Japanese village in the middle of the night on an old fishing boat, still in her elegant signature St. John suit and high heels. On the small fishing boat, Gable took the time to appreciate the traditional culture and understand the community. It was her ability to build relationships with families that enabled Gable to bring people together on a basic human level and create a strong relationship on behalf of the U.S. "Whether it was sitting with my high heels in the middle of night fishing or my daughter drawing a picture and writing a thank you note," laughed Gable, she was able to create a sense of family, community, and human connection that crossed cultural divides.

After the World's Fair, Gable was recognized on the Senate floor for pioneering a different, successful business model based on inclusive solutions that successfully enabled U.S. participation in the event.

Gender diversity positively impacts economics as well. At the 2019 World Economic Forum's Annual Meeting in Davos, Standard & Poor (S&P) shared estimated numbers of economic gain if the labor force participation rate of women were equal to the rate of men. According to the numbers, the U.S. economy would grow by 8.7 percent, the French economy by 17 percent, and the Japanese economy by 14 percent.[65]

CEO of Grant Thornton Australia Greg Keith says, "Diversity is not a women's issue. Women get it. They live with it every day. Change happens when leaders take action. So, I want to have a conversation with the men in the room. Embrace it and own it."[66] According to Keith, gender inclusiveness is a two-way street.

---

65   Laura D'Andrea Tyson, "Gender Parity Can Boost Economic Growth. Here's How," World Economic Forum, March 8, 2019.

66   "Women in Business: Building a Blueprint for Action," Grant Thornton International, March 2019.

From Finland to Albania, to the U.S. and Japan, women use inclusiveness to build coalitions, facilitate diplomacy, create connections, and improve peaceful security. Diversity around the table does not refer solely to cognitive differences—background, culture, race, religion, and gender all play significant roles. These factors are instrumental to cultivating diversity of thought and enabling the inclusion of women and their unique skillsets.

CHAPTER 10

THE ART OF RELATIONSHIP BUILDING

———

"Always be more than you appear and never appear to be more than you are."

—ANGELA MERKEL

FIRST WOMAN CHANCELLOR OF GERMANY

Relationship building is the heartbeat of diplomacy. It's what enables foreign service officers to create strong policy, tactfully negotiate, and successfully represent their country. A diplomat's appearance represents how their country appears. A diplomat's rhetoric reflects his or her nation's rhetoric. A diplomat's relationship building is indicative of that nation's relationship building. My conversations with diplomats taught me how relationship building is not a science, but rather an art. I have seen this in my own work. Creating a unique connection takes sincerity, curiosity, persistence, understanding, and, oftentimes, grace. People should want to talk with you, be around you, and see it as beneficial to know you. Successful diplomats possess a particularly keen ability to build these relationships on behalf of their country to ensure security and to advance policy.

Sheryl Shum saw the benefit of relationship building early in her diplomatic career. After graduating from the University of Chicago with a focus in economics and international relations, she joined Singapore's Foreign Ministry. She was a "real rookie" who found herself at the negotiating table, discussing border issues with her nation's neighbors. The discussions pertained to maritime issues, boundary negotiations, and piracy. Her team was led by a woman who became one of her first mentors in the foreign service.

With dark hair and a petite frame, she enters a room in a dignified fashion. Throughout many interactions, I've seen how small session briefings, large events, and arranging her country's national day celebration have transformed Shum into a highly-skilled diplomat. She was promoted to Deputy Chief of Mission in the middle of her posting in Washington.

During a sabbatical to get her graduate degree at the University of California in Berkeley, we speak over the phone about her fifteen years of diplomatic training and how she continues to grow. She tells me how when she was in high school, reading Former Secretary Madeleine Albright's autobiography inspired her to seek a career in foreign policy and diplomacy. She remembers being inspired by a woman's ability to rise to that position. At the time, woman Ambassador Chan Heng Chee represented Singapore in Washington from

July 1996 to July 2012—quite a run! Seeing these women in leadership motivated Shum's professional trajectory.

Shum tells me that observing Ambassador Chee "doing high power work, and still retaining what essentially makes you a woman" was powerful. She recalls how Ambassador Chee and the other women in Singapore's Foreign Ministry were able to "move with charm, using culture, intuition, and empathy" while reaching out to stakeholders. They were adept at building relationships with male counterparts as well as their male counterparts' spouses. This inclusive approach to relationship building was truly effective.

Shum shares, "Diplomacy is about human relations. It's not just about the business of it, it's about the soft skills, and how you approach a person." It's about the personal relationship, and Shum sees how women are curiously skilled in speaking to individuals on that level.

In contemplating on a surface level of what women bring to diplomacy, Shum says most people envision women working on "'women issues' like gender issues, human rights issues, issues about children, protection, discrimination," and so on. In the current era, women are starting to realize that "We don't need to pigeonhole ourselves into those roles." Yes, Shum agrees that women are natural caregivers and empathetic, but that these are not the only strengths of women diplomats. With the art of relationship building, women stand shoulder to shoulder in the toughest negotiations.

Shum is of the opinion that women bring "charisma and flair" to diplomatic interactions. She says these soft skills, including knowledge about personal relationships, are vital. "You're dealing with foreign policy, which is a tough subject, but you're approaching it with humanity," she notes. That's one of the reasons Shum strongly believes women are suited for diplomacy.

While serving as a woman in the foreign service, Shum discovered what she calls a "global sisterhood." The connection she has shared with other women diplomats during her time in Washington has only strengthened, and she says the sisterhood seeks each other out in these contexts.

On the phone, Shum reflected that there's "so much change in the world right now." She actively looks for opportunities to bring her accrued knowledge to the table in addition to the new knowledge she continues to acquire.

The job is a constant relocation whirlwind for Shum. She emphasizes the importance of building relationships wherever she goes. During her time in Washington, she started questioning whether she should continue her career in diplomacy. While she doesn't have her own family, Shum says the constant moving puts a toll on one's personal life. She has been able to build professional relationships, but personal relationships required to build a family are challenging.

Shum discusses how she sought the counsel of her Ambassador in Washington to discuss the longevity of diplomatic careers. She tells me that diplomats learn only through years of training and investment by their home country. Shum sees her work with a sense of duty, and her Ambassador reminded her of why she wanted to work in the field in the first place.

Shum candidly emphasizes, "Diplomacy is something that you don't learn in school, you learn on the job."

Shum was initially brought to her to seat at the table by a colleague who asked her to moderate a discussion between two ambassadors. The "sisterhood" brought her in, Shum pulled up a chair, and through the experience, she began to develop "own her voice."

At the end of her posting as Deputy Chief of Mission in Washington, Shum was asked to host an event on women in diplomacy. She jumped at the chance to provide a mentorship and exposure opportunity for her women colleagues. She invited them to present on the panel about women in Singapore's history, the Embassy's public diplomacy, and how Singapore builds public policy. While Shum understood the importance of building relationships outside the Embassy, she also understands the importance of relationships with her colleagues and her responsibility to mentor and support them. Together, they formed the panel. Instead of just speaking alone on behalf of Singapore, she invited her women colleagues to the table.

Shum is especially proud of that event because she sees sharing the spotlight to build the confidence of her peers and sharing her expertise as integral parts of leadership building. Shum herself was invited by a senior leader and reaped the benefits of being brought to the table. When it was Shum's turn, she was ready to nurture participation from colleagues who otherwise would not have been given a chance to share their voice.

Shum tells me about the hierarchical nature of diplomacy. She has seen how some women diplomats feel they need an invitation to speak and how men diplomats don't seem to have that problem. Shum remains conscious of this inequity, and she feels that's why it is important to ask women colleagues in the back of the room for their input. The importance of bringing people along with you rather than elbowing them out of a seat at the table is something she has learned in her time in Washington.

She has seen the art of building relationships firsthand and has been "the beneficiary" of it as well. Giving back by bringing others to the table is part of her mantra.

According to a Harvard Business Review article, "The reality is that just as women benefit from male mentors, sponsors, and allies, men also gain from the mentorship, leadership, and sponsorship of women."[67] To build relationships and facilitate gender-balanced teams, women leaders must also invest in mentoring male colleagues.

For relationship building, there must be a certain level of confidence in oneself. "Confidence comes from competence. And there is no shortcut for competence," Shum says. Knowing the policy issues, doing your "homework," and showing up prepared when you get to the table all work together to create opportunities for success. Shum stresses the importance of this point: "Do your work and prepare. And once you show up at the table, be confident that you have prepared, and own your voice."

---

67 Rania H. Anderson, "Challenging Our Gendered Idea of Mentorship," *Harvard Business Review,* January 6, 2020.

While Shum rejects the notion that she needs an invitation to speak, she continues to challenge herself and other women colleagues. "If you have something important to say, you don't necessarily have to wait to be invited," she says. Many diplomats interviewed for this book stress that if a foreign service representative doesn't speak, their country doesn't speak and thus isn't represented. As national representatives, diplomats don't have the luxury of waiting for an invitation. This responsibility pushes diplomats out of their comfort zone to fulfill the responsibility of building relationships and using their voice.

* * *

While the art of diplomacy doesn't change, the face of diplomacy does, especially in Finland. In December 2019, thirty-four-year-old Sanna Marin became the world's youngest Prime Minister. In this role, she formed a coalition government in which all five party leaders were women and the majority were under the age of forty. (Please hold your applause—there's more.) In Finland's cabinet, twelve portfolios are represented by women, and only seven are represented by men. Lastly, nearly half (around 47 percent) of the country's parliamentarians are women.

Two factors have contributed to Finland's high economic and political participation of women: health and education.[68] And these women are making an impact. Under Prime Minister Marin's leadership, Finland is working on closing the gender pay gap, encouraging men to take parental leave,

---

68   Carmen Niethammer, "Finland's New Government Is Young And Led By Women—Here's What The Country Does To Promote Diversity," *Forbes*, December 12, 2019.

discussing the idea of a four-day work week for families to have more time together, and pledging to address climate change by becoming carbon neutral by 2035.[69] And it is certain that the accomplishment of any or all of those goals will require relationship building.

One of my favorite photos of Finland shows bikes parked on heavy snow. Finns are ardent cyclists regardless of the weather. Finnish Ambassador Kirsti Kauppi is no exception. Kauppi has taken her enjoyment of biking with her from her hometown of Oulu, Northern Finland, to posts all around the world as a career diplomat. In addition to her native Finnish, she is fluent in Swedish, German, French, and English.

Kauppi has built quite a distinguished career. She completed her master's degree in economics at Finland's Helsinki School of Economics and Business Administration in 1981. Two years later, she joined the Ministry of Foreign Affairs. During her time at the Ministry, Kauppi has been placed in Vienna, Berlin, Washington, Brussels, Helsinki, and Bangkok. Her positions have ranged from Ambassador, Deputy Chief of Mission, Head of the Political Department as well as the department for Africa and the Middle East, to advisor to the Secretary of State.

In spite of her strong portfolio, Kauppi is unassuming in stature and has a lightness about her. Although it may seem her career path has had a certain trajectory, Kauppi says the opposite was true. She says that she "never had that kind of

---

69 Lisa Abend, "Finland's Sanna Marin, the World's Youngest Female Head of Government, Wants Equality, Not Celebrity," *Time*, accessed February 2, 2020.

ambition and didn't think about positions"—rather, she was simply "enthusiastic" about her jobs and created relationships along the way. "I loved the issues, and for me, it was very motivating to just work with the issues. I didn't think about a career in that sense," Kauppi shares. Her secret is that "you don't have to be ambitious as far as your career is concerned, but it is important to be passionate about the work you do."

On my way to our meeting, I walk up two wooden spiraling staircases and through an ordinary wood door to Ambassador Kauppi's office in Washington. She invites me to sit down, and I ask where. (The options are a long couch and modern chairs.) She says, "Wherever—none of the options are that comfortable."

Finns are known for their directness, as Kauppi tells me during our interview. During our conversation in this modern office, her voice wavers. At one point, Kauppi describes her voice as vocally "weak," but I find her far from weak. The woman I interview is insightful, direct, and thoughtful, with a type of kindness that shines throughout our conversation.

Though there were fewer women in leadership positions at the beginning of her career, Kauppi remembers women in the foreign ministry and recalls gender equality was a part of the professional environment. Despite that, however, she has had her fair share of moments in which she or a woman colleague speaks during a meeting and no one seems to listen. Then a male colleague will make the same statement, "and suddenly everybody says yes, exactly." She says this partially in jest but is also serious. "Almost all of us women in low or leadership positions recognize that experience." Most of the women diplomats I interviewed shared similar sentiments and experiences. Though we joke, it is an unfortunate, infamous reality.

To bring people together, a leader must be themselves. Even laughing during serious situations can provide much-needed levity, according to Kauppi. As she puts it, there are different ways of "being" for different situations. She believes it is important for diplomats to remember that you cannot "behave contrary to what you are." Trying to embody a persona that is unnatural is ineffective. It actually makes a person more vulnerable, because they lack the foundation of being true to themselves.

During our conversation, I realized that most of Kauppi's opinions are about culture instead of gender. Understanding the culture is critical to relationship building. Understanding gender in culture is another layer. Learning from different kinds of people cultivates diversity of thought, and staying within homogeneous cultures reinforces people's opinions and biases. According to Kauppi, male-dominated gatherings tend to exhibit a certain culture, as do very female-dominated gatherings. Kauppi says, "breaking [this] uniformity is important."

Kauppi believes diversity is a very obvious strength. That said, even with diversity there has to be an element of commonality to "set the foundation."

Early in her career and at a young age, Kauppi was in charge of development projects in Eastern Africa. On her first trip to negotiate projects with local authorities, she discovered a new approach to improving a particular project. It was quite a sight, Kauppi says, as she was only twenty-five years old at the time and "even smaller and shyer than today."

At the table, it became clear to Kauppi that there was a relatively big group on the opposing side. Although everyone was "nice," she was a young woman presenting an idea and the group was somewhat "dismissive." Despite perfunctory responses from the group, she continued to push her ideas. When negotiations ended, a group participant told her boss that it was impressive to see how Kauppi pursued her thinking in front of everyone to get the desired solution and result. Kauppi's boss shared the compliment with her. This, she says, was a decisive moment—that acknowledgment took her "leaps ahead" in her confidence and in trusting her own approach to solutions.

Being granted this responsibility at an early stage and throughout her career allowed Kauppi to experience how to build relationships within different cultures. She says that giving team members individual responsibilities helps them grow into leaders. They may negotiate situations differently, but this real-world experience encourages them to grow wings and fly.

Working in both African and Asian cultures at such a young age helped Kauppi. Due to the age barrier between her and others, she says, respect is not a given. Age deems respect. That said, exercising "authority and responsibility" in such situations gives young professionals the ability to embody confidence in relationship building.

While Kauppi is now at the pinnacle of her career as the top Finnish diplomat in Washington, she admits she still doubts herself. She thinks this feeling is more common among women than men. "I'm not very self-assured at all. I'm especially bad in that respect," she says quietly.

I must admit astonishment at Kauppi's statement that she has never really grown out of her lack of self-confidence and feels she has held herself back. She confides that she could have done more and could be even more productive, had she not "doubted herself all the time." This recurring theme leads me to recognize the prevalence of self-doubt in all layers of leadership. This doubt blocks us all from building relationships and confidence.

Kauppi says she combats this self-doubt with encouragement from people she respects. Relationship building and mutual respect create more confidence in yourself, as well as the ability to embrace or trust the other person's encouragement or guidance.

Kauppi notes that the opposite is true as well. The example she shares is from her time as Ambassador in Washington. She recalls being among a small group discussing politics—a classic pastime in the city. Kauppi offered her opinion, and an older gentleman she admired asked her in front of the group, "Kirsti, did you think about that yourself?"

He doubted her thinking—publicly. She didn't respond. Put-downs from someone you admire or respect, especially in a group setting, can be just as impactful as praise.

Elevating a colleague's point in a sincere way is as important to relationship building as showing appreciation, especially between differing cultures. "Even if somebody says something dumb, it's important to appreciate it," Kauppi says, claiming it is always possible to respond with encouragement. For example, "It's good that you made the point. I fully disagree, but it's great you made the point."

One question Kauppi hears frequently is whether women should change their way of talking, interacting, or taking space in the context of building cross-cultural relationships. She believes that "Everybody should be able to be there, to be heard and listened to, and understood as they are." You don't have to be a "bulldozer" that knocks other people down or shrink for someone else's comfort. Neither one aids in relationship building.

Kauppi believes in the importance of "learn[ing] from your colleagues and appreciate[ing] them." She says that finding colleagues—both "lower and higher in the hierarchy with whom you can sound out your ideas and thinking to broaden your horizons"—will develop a diplomat's capabilities. Just like any relationship, Kauppi says, "You cannot do it alone."

Kauppi rejects the notion that women must strive for leadership positions for the sake of equality. Rather, she thinks that people can contribute regardless of whether they are in leadership positions. That said, she "know[s] the problem is often that in leadership, we don't have enough women." Research from 2019 states that 29 percent of senior management roles globally are held by women; while this is still a minority, it is the highest number on record.[70]

The art of building relationships and networking go hand in hand. Though Kauppi believes networking is very important, she says it is also "very important to be true to yourself." She says that striving for the top leadership position, especially as you are building a relationship, is sometimes "a little bit of a false objective." People do not have to be in leadership

---

70 "Women in Management: Quick Take," Catalyst, August 7, 2019.

positions to meet their "highest potential," contribute to a solution, or "be at their best." Kauppi firmly believes that all levels of hierarchy in diplomacy are valuable.

As she leads her team, Kauppi sees that the "younger female generations are more demanding vis-à-vis themselves." It's an old story—according to Kauppi—that women want to be what she calls "100 percent." It represents this idea of perfection. Kauppi explains, "It's not a very productive attitude towards yourself to always expect to be 100 percent."

I hear about this burden in my friend groups. The goal of striving for everything—career, family, and a sense of belonging—is pervasive. None of us are ever at 100 percent. Building relationships, not only in diplomacy but in all aspects of life, takes imperfection, not perfection.

The expectation of perfection and the focus on our shortcomings hold us back. According to Kauppi, to get rid of the burden of striving for 100 percent, you must build your network of support and relationships.

My mind traces back to the image of Kauppi riding a bike. All the gears, wheels, and systems must work together to propel a cyclist forward. It's not perfect. One shift or a quick change can cause the bike to wobble. Even the most proficient bike riders lose their balance every so often. By gaining confidence and understanding that if you fall, it is ok, you can get back on and keep riding.

CHAPTER 11

RAISE YOUR HAND, RAISE YOUR VOICE

———

"Trust yourself. Create the kind of self that you will be happy to live with all your life."

—GOLDA MEIR

FIRST WOMAN PRIME MINISTER OF ISRAEL

If you wish to change the lens of diplomacy, raise your hand and raise your voice—no one will do it for you. Knowing how and when to do so is a key component of emotional intelligence. As mentioned in Part 2 of the book, emotional intelligence tends to be a strong trait among women. As a diplomat working on systemic geopolitical issues, Ambassador Ursula Plassnik uses both emotional intelligence and analytical thinking. You can hear it in the tone of her voice, see it in her eyes, and feel it in her presence.

Plassnik's work led her to meeting and bonding with women across the globe from "entirely different backgrounds and living conditions," varying income levels, socioeconomic upbringings, cultures, races, and religions. However, she has noticed a single shared experience—"We all experienced not having been taken seriously." When she meets with women groups, Plassnik finds this common similarity to be an asset in creating "immediate closeness with women audiences across the globe."

Plassnik describes her career as a "sequence of unexpected challenges," not strategically "planned steps." She typically served as the strategic thinker in the room—a "grey mouse behind battalions of ambitious men on the frontline." Coincidentally, she shares that it took a man to force her out of her professional comfort zone.

Plassnik's colleague—an Austrian Vice Chancellor and later Prime Minister—encouraged her to develop her leadership capacity by appointing her as his Chief of Staff. She describes her time in that position as a "rough road" and "not much of a pleasure trip." While simultaneously handling multiple responsibilities and competing priorities, Plassnik learned how to communicate with any level of power or position. She says this lesson taught her how to "feel and speak at eye level with any man or woman." This served as a pivotal turning point in her career as she ventured from diplomacy to politics.

Plassnik stands out in a crowd due to her height, and she proves that difference matters. She advises that for both women and men in leadership positions, "If you want to make a difference, dare to differ both in substance and in style!" She believes a diplomat's or leader's greatest assets in representing a country are their unique ideas and presence.

Plassnik quotes Mahatma Gandhi: "First they ignore you, then they laugh at you, then they fight you, then you win." She believes that this attitude gives anyone the ability to enter a confrontation, endure it, and ultimately prevail. Some call it endurance, while others say it is resilience. Either way, Plassnik believes this is the real meaning of leadership through the lens of foreign relations. However, you also have to cope with the fact you may feel lonely at the top. You may find yourself the odd woman or odd man out. Sometimes in life, according to Plassnik, "The moment of leadership is the moment of loneliness." Anyone upwardly mobile must understand that the further up the leadership chain they climb, the lonelier it gets, but the view from the top provides a vaster and better vantage point.

* * *

You'll recall Lauren Protentis from Chapter 9 and her work in building a communications framework to defeat ISIS. Though she strides into a room with airy confidence and charm today, she says she wasn't always this way. During her time with the U.S. State Department, Protentis worked tirelessly to grow her professional network and advance her career.

Protentis shares that a pivotal turning point in her career was realizing she lacked the courage and confidence to stand up for herself in the workplace. In dealing with tough bosses, she knew she skirted a fine line between reporting gender bias and needing their support and authority for program funding and promotions. She felt confused, intimidated, and disempowered, and the experience shook her confidence.

Protentis spent time reflecting on what she could have done differently to better endure this treatment or get promoted. Over time, she realized that the problem wasn't her at all. She did succeed in accomplishing a tremendous goal, and she made a significant impact in the realm of communications and national security. Her idea effectively built a network from the ground-up. No one could take that away from her and her team.

Today, Protentis encourages others in the field of diplomacy and any sector to push back when needed. "Know your rights. Don't be intimidated by power, seniority, uniforms, or male figures. Stand your ground and never let anyone shake your confidence. No one can challenge what you know or your story," she declares. "Each achievement and experience is part of your unique capability."

Protentis and I meet at the exclusive Georgetown-based club "The Wing," a gathering spot catering to women in the workforce with ergonomically designed furniture, plush champagne and rose hues, and lots of natural light. Over coffee, she shares that she was originally terrified when taking a seat "at the table." Most policy wonks, Washingtonians, and diplomats understand what having a seat at the table means, especially in terms of negotiating agreements.

Protentis continues to grow in this regard. She confesses that every day during her department's senior meeting, she makes a point to not apologize. Instead, she takes her seat at the table. She feels it sends a clear message about her importance in the space. She has noticed that most of the time, when someone walks into the room and the table is full, it is a woman who gives up her seat. If someone walks in the room that is more senior than her and is looking around for a seat, she is no longer the woman who moves. And she doesn't apologize for it.

"Women need to stop giving up their seats . . . because it's detrimental to our ability to lead, command, and for others to take us seriously," Protentis explains.

I always know when Protentis is in the room—a trait that will hold her in good stead. I jokingly tell her that when and if she runs for office, I want to be on her team. More importantly, I'm thankful she is starting to share these stories. Women in the foreign service need to know they are not alone—that they can assert themselves and take their seats at the table.

The views expressed above are her own and not those of the U.S. Government.

* * *

While some women need to fight for a seat at the table, other women come from cultures where there isn't the same struggle. Although September 2017 marked the first time Sweden sent a woman Ambassador to Washington, the country has championed gender equality for many years.

Swedish Ambassador Karin Olofsdotter was not new to Washington upon receiving her post, as she previously served as Deputy Chief of Mission from 2008 to 2011. She also was not new to the position of Ambassador, having served in Hungary from 2011 to 2014. Ironically, Olofsdotter never thought she would work for the foreign service. She grew up in the south of Sweden as the only child of two parents from "simple backgrounds." Her mother was a hard worker who owned a women's shoe store in a town of about 100,000 people. Her father was also in the shoe business as a traveling salesman and spent time taking care of her when he wasn't traveling. When she was seventeen, Olofsdotter spent a year as an exchange student in Egg Harbor Township, New Jersey, near Atlantic City. Little did she know that years later, she would represent her country among the American people.

While studying at the University of Lund in Sweden, Olofsdotter also spent eight months abroad in Moscow in addition to a year at the UCLA Anderson School of Management. She also spent half a year in New Zealand bartending in her early twenties and meeting different people.[71]

Olofsdotter remembers how Sweden suffered a huge economic crisis in the '90s. When she sought career opportunities, she found that "There were no jobs. Zero." The Ministry advertised the diplomatic training program and she applied. With her background in Russian from studying abroad, Olofsdotter was accepted. Of the 2,000 applicants, she was chosen for a class of twenty future foreign service officers.

Olofsdotter entered the foreign service in 1994 as one of two women in the group who spoke Russian, in addition to three or four men. Both she and her friend questioned whether they would be posted to Russia, fearing the men

---

71   Matt Bewig, "Ambassador of Sweden to the United States: Who Is Karin Olofsdotter?," AllGov, December 3, 2017.

would get the post to help with military service learning. However, Olofsdotter was posted to Moscow and her friend to St. Petersburg.

During her time in Russia—a formative post for her career—Olofsdotter had a boss who would see her and remark, "Here comes the sunshine of the Embassy." While she thinks he meant it positively and nicely, it was also "a bit derogatory, sexist, and diminishing." Would he have said that to a male employee of the same age? She equates this to a generational shift and a sign of how social norms have drastically changed since the '90s.

I sit with Olofsdotter and her press secretary as Olofsdotter shares how much she loves her job. It's a sunny afternoon in late September, and her corner office boasts a sweeping view of the Potomac River. Complete with a cream-colored couch and a white office table, the neutral office style is a blend of Restoration Hardware and IKEA. Olofsdotter and her candid demeanor are fitting in this airy, peaceful space. The slight jovial smirk makes her both captivating and approachable. Olofsdotter's press secretary notes how the Ambassador's manner invites people in.

Early in the conversation, Olofsdotter declares, "I'm very proud of my country. And I love representing it, because I think we have found a good way of life." While she notes that Sweden has its flaws, it's a dignified system on the whole. She feels fortunate to have found a career that is always evolving. Every three to four years, she changes jobs and "gets to learn something new."

More so, the foreign service has shown Olofsdotter firsthand how gender equity might be achieved in all sectors. She says,

"Personally, I think that all jobs are better if they have equal representation and different kinds of people, because if you just have one type of people, it's less creative and doesn't bring as much experience." Cultivating a diverse group of professionals is beneficial in any field.

In working predominantly on security and foreign policy, Olofsdotter feels that she and her fellow women colleagues were always taken seriously. She views being a woman in the field of security as an advantage. As she puts it, "If you're good at what you do, and you stick out in a crowd, that's good."

One of Olofsdotter's learned leadership tactics is to "strike first." When negotiating in Brussels, she made sure to speak at least second or third to set the tone for the agenda. It's a helpful negotiation style, especially to those of the gender or racial minority in the room. She tells woman leaders to raise their hands and raise their voices. If you speak early, she says, you can open the conversation and lead the discussion. Speaking first also assures you are listened to.

As Director-General of Trade, Olofsdotter has found many countries in Sweden's neighborhood to have similar policies and positions. But Olofsdotter also says that after speaking first on behalf of her country, other representatives would say, "Oh, we just echo Sweden." This tactic sends the message that "people see you as an active and influential person, even though the other ones had the same stance." In a way, it's a strategy for "owning" the room. And anyone of any background can utilize this skill.

Olofsdotter says the turning point of her career was during her maternity leave with her first child. In the Swedish foreign service, everyone typically rotates in September. She was going back to work in March, and there weren't many jobs available mid-season. The job the government had open for her was "boring." She recalls thinking, "If I have to do that job, I will become a nasty person." Olofsdotter is a firm believer in needing to do work that's enjoyable.

One of Olofsdotter's friends from her early diplomatic training days was the head of the minister's office. The Foreign Minister of Sweden has a civil servant diplomat recruited and assigned to them in a nonpolitical appointment.

In October, Olofsdotter called her friend to meet for coffee. Her friend whispered on the phone, "I haven't thought about you. Are you interested in the job as the private diplomat to the State Secretary for Foreign Affairs?" Her friend urged Olofsdotter to come in for an interview. She did, and she got the job, ultimately serving as Chief of Staff to several Swedish Foreign Ministers and as Director of the Minister's Office in Stockholm. This connection led Olofsdotter to years of experience with political leaders, as Chief of Staff in a social democratic government and then through a conservative government. Those years propelled Olofsdotter's career forward. She reflects on that one phone call and believes many things in life happen by chance, so it's important to just go for it. "We can strategize about what we want to do, but it's very much about taking an opportunity when it comes by."

Olofsdotter worries about the younger generations as she watches her children become teenagers. "I think this new generation of millennials and onwards [are] called the perfect generation, as [in] everything should be perfect—your home should be perfect, you should look perfect, [and] grades should be perfect." Olofsdotter says that it seems certain age groups won't take risks or chances because of this standard of perfection. She's concerned that these future generation will lose out because they don't jump on chance opportunities. Raising your hand and raising your voice requires taking risks.

In our conversation, Olofsdotter says she fully recognizes the difference between men and women. The Ministry's Head of Personnel has a harder time recruiting women to managerial positions. A woman will read a list of seven qualifications and say, "I only have five or six, I can't apply." A man will say, "I fit two, that job is for me!" Raising your hand, raising your voice, taking a chance, and believing in yourself are crucial to this work. Olofsdotter says we need to place greater trust in our abilities. While she shared it's a generalization of a trend, this situation is "the Achilles heel for women."

In our discussion, Olofsdotter insists on taking opportunities as they come and envisioning the possibilities, but she also cautions against reflecting for too long and missing opportunities. This applies to both a person's work life and personal life.

Olofsdotter says that the more women pursue challenges and climb the ladder of success, the less their gender is questioned. "Who would question Angela Merkel or Indira Gandhi?" she asks. Their politics might be questioned, Olofsdotter says, but "they're not questioned [with regard to gender] because they are women who have become the highest leaders of their land."

Gender equality through the lens of Swedish culture is much different than in other cultures. From Africa to the United States, cultural context matters. And no matter the culture, raising your hand and raising your voice are 100 percent the first steps in taking a stand for your beliefs or your country.

CHAPTER 12

IMPACT FROM OPPORTUNITY

———

"No nation can meet the world's challenges alone."

—HILLARY RODHAM CLINTON
FORMER U.S. SECRETARY OF STATE AND
FIRST WOMAN NOMINATED TO BE A U.S.
PRESIDENT BY A MAJOR POLITICAL PARTY

My many conversations with women diplomats have revealed that regardless of their homogeneous or diverse origins, everyone agreed that increasing diversity around the table is integral to building peace. Giving people the opportunity to lead was more complicated.

Iceland is an apt example of a historically homogeneous population with its secluded geographic location. However, the populace has evolved. In 2018, the population was 350,000[72] and in 2019, 50,000 of its inhabitants were immigrants.[73] The culture of Iceland is changing.

In mid-December, I visit the Embassy of Iceland in Washington, which is located in the same building as the Embassy of Sweden. I sit in the "IKEA suite" that looks like a sophisticated showroom. This modern, light, and fresh space overlooks the Potomac River. I'm told the "small" suite serves as a visitor's apartment; that said, it's much larger than my own apartment, and the view is quite different than my city alley of crisscrossing cables.

I originally meet Ambassador Bergdís Ellertsdóttir of Iceland at a "women in diplomacy" event hosted by *The Washington Diplomat*. After the panel, I patiently wait for the swarm of people to disperse so I can ask her if she'd be interested in being interviewed for the book. She warmly welcomes the opportunity.

Ellertsdóttir has light eyes, dark hair, and a modest and peaceful disposition. During our interview, she sits on a modern couch in the IKEA suite with a notepad and pen while her fluffy, foaming coffee cools.

Ellertsdóttir was born in 1962 and grew up during a time when Iceland faced a lack of housing. Her family moved into a new suburban area with high rises. She tells me she didn't know any diplomats growing up—and in her homogenous culture,

---

72 "Population of Iceland Has Now Topped 350,000: Immigrants Make Up 11.3% of Population," *Iceland Magazine*, May 2, 2018.

73 Vala Hafstað, "More than 50,000 Immigrants in Iceland," *Iceland Monitor*, December 2, 2019.

she knew little about the world. Reading sparked her interest, and because there were few women leaders and politicians to serve as role models, the characters in her books became her inspiration. Ellertsdóttir followed the stories of strong women such as Beverly Gray and Nancy Drew. She tells me, "I lived in the library and it opened up the world to me."

Life changed in 1980 when Iceland elected its first woman president, Vigdís Finnbogadóttir. She was also the world's first woman to be elected as Head of State. Ellertsdóttir says this election "changed everything." As she puts it, "There was now this woman role model for generations and generations." Finnbogadóttir served for sixteen years as President to Iceland, and her leadership sent a ripple of change throughout the country. More women were appointed to Iceland's Parliament, and they were elected without the use of a quota system in addition to being ensured parental leave, subsidized daycare, and a refocus on the gender pay gap.

Inspired by Finnbogadóttir, Ellertsdóttir enrolled in college at the University of Freiburg in Germany in 1982 and studied German, political science, English, and history. She continued at the University of Iceland and graduated in 1987. She then attended the University of Essex in the U.K. completing her master of arts in European studies in 1989.

Ellertsdóttir's work ethic and expertise created many opportunities for her. Little did she know that she would have a diplomatic career spanning NATO, the European Free Trade Association, the European Union, and serve as Iceland's Ambassador to Belgium, the Netherlands, Luxembourg, Switzerland, San Marino, and the U.S.

Ellertsdóttir originally joined the Foreign Ministry in 1991 and worked in the trade department. She recalls being one of the few women working at the Ministry headquarters. All the leadership positions such as ministers and above were held by men. She says, "In general, Iceland is a very equal society with gender equality, and we always score very high on international indexes of gender parity. But foreign ministries seem to be more traditional, authoritarian, and old fashion[ed]. I think change has come later to diplomacy compared to other sectors."

Ellertsdóttir tells me she didn't see significant change until the year 2000. It happened to be the same year Iceland introduced the first individual and non-transferable paternity leave. This gave three months of leave to each individual parent, plus an extra three months to the couple to share as they chose. This policy change shifted male attitudes, according to Ellertsdóttir, as fathers went from having two weeks paid parental leave to three months! The policy aimed to make both parents equal caretakers of a child. "[The policy] blurs out any differences between the sexes. If you hired a young man, he was just as likely to take off time as a woman when a child was born," she explains.

Since the year 2000, around 74 to 90 percent of fathers have taken paternity leave.[74] The encouraged use of paternity leave creates an environment that socially accepts fathers as caretakers. A 2012 report on gender equality in Iceland noted that since the policy, parents, especially fathers, had

---

74   Dwyer Gunn, "How Should Parental Leave Be Structured? Ask Iceland," *Slate*, April 3, 2013.

closer relationships with their children and provided more gender equality in the workplace.[75] Iceland even passed a law increasing the parental leave for private and public sectors to twelve months with five months non-transferable to each parent and two months decided between the couple.

A PhD student at the University of Iceland interviewed young Icelandic men who were not yet fathers about masculinity and femininity. They shared that they see paternal leave and child-care participation as natural parts of masculinity,[76] which also demonstrates a departure from traditional attitudes.

Ellertsdóttir tells me that the policy in the Ministry and government also encourages a better work-life balance. She says, "If people such as high-ranking ministers decide not to take leave, people are outraged." Ellertsdóttir now sees all parents, regardless of gender, aiding in childcare, whether by leaving work to pick up a sick child from school or attending their child's extracurricular activity. Chapter 14 elaborates on this topic, as many countries strive to integrate policies that support work-life balance.

The Prime Minister of Iceland, Katrín Jakobsdóttir, wrote that universal quality childcare and funded parental leave address historic "systematic discrimination" and transform women's opportunities to participate in society.[77]

75 "Gender Equality in Iceland: Information on Gender Issues in Iceland," The Center for Gender Equality Iceland, February 2012.

76 Ingólfur V. Gíslason, "Parental Leave in Iceland Gives Dad a Strong Position," Nordic Labour Journal, April 12, 2019.

77 Katrín Jakobsdóttir, "How to Build a Paradise for Women. A Lesson from Iceland," World Economic Forum, November 23, 2018.

Ellertsdóttir recalls a change in the Foreign Ministry around 2002, when the permanent Secretary of State—the highest public servant in the Ministry—focused his initiatives on gender equality. He decided to change the structure of the Ministry to have only two pillars: economic and political.

He appointed two women to lead each pillar and report directly to him. Ellertsdóttir was appointed to lead the political pillar, which focused on political and security issues. At the time, she was in her early forties and leading multiple departments that included men much older than her. She divulges that she was afraid men might "make her life difficult" or refuse to listen to her. On the contrary, her male colleagues were respectful and cooperative. She says, "This leadership experience gave me the confidence to become the person I am today."

Two thoughts come to my mind while she spoke:

1. **Leadership sets the tone.** The influence of top leadership, such as the permanent Secretary of State, provides the needed support for change. It is imperative that top leaders promote gender parity and equality in the system.

2. **Employees need the space to lead.** Learning experience is a crucial part of training. Providing leadership opportunities early in careers empowers individuals and grants them the skills to work collaboratively and learn from multiple levels of an organization.

Iceland's first woman Minister for Foreign Affairs, Valgerður Sverrisdóttir, served from 2006 to 2007. From 2007 to 2009,

Ingibjörg Sólrún Gísladóttir, became Foreign Minister. In 2007, Ellertsdóttir became the Director-General for International Security and Development. She relays to me how different it was to work for a woman Foreign Minister. She recalls the Foreign Minister being more receptive and open to ideas by genuinely listening. "You would think listening is something that happens all the time, but I have seen many leaders who come in and think they know it all," shares Ellertsdóttir.

With the Foreign Minister, Ellertsdóttir worked on development cooperation. They focused on women empowerment in Africa and formally visited Uganda and South Africa. The Ministry delegation happened to be all women. Ellertsdóttir says, "We met with many amazing African women who had small companies, and I don't think we would have done that with a man as minister. The focus on gender would not have been woven into the policy. A male delegation or minister may have focused on other aspects of development cooperation," she quietly emphasizes.

During that time, Ellertsdóttir was involved in the development of a list of Icelandic women who were willing to be at the table and had the right experience for peace negotiations and other critical decision making skills. It was part of a Nordic coalition to combat the stereotype of "there are no women out there who can or want to do this work."

Gender-focused policies are now a unifying thread of diplomacy and negotiation that started within the development cooperation Ellertsdóttir worked on.

From 2007 to 2012, Ellertsdóttir was appointed Deputy Secretary General of the European Free Trade Association in Brussels. In 2012, she served as Chief Negotiator in the Iceland-China Free Trade Agreement. In 2014, Iceland sent her as the representative to the European Union, and she also served as Ambassador to Belgium, the Netherlands, Luxembourg, Switzerland, and San Marino.

While Ellertsdóttir appreciates having the opportunity to engage in impactful work for her country, she laments seeing photos from meetings about NATO, security, trade, or economics in which only men are pictured and only two ethnicities or races are represented. Until there is truly gender parity and diversity around the table, Ellertsdóttir believes it's important to persist in advocating for it.

From 2018 to 2019, Ellertsdóttir served as the permanent representative of Iceland to the UN in New York. She took part in resolution discussions about women and security. Through her work, she hears testimonies of women from conflict areas who have survived sexual violence. She says, "I heard from these brave young women who had been kidnapped from their families and raped. Their experiences were so horrific, they were hard to even listen to. I wanted to go out screaming and do something about it."

Listening to these stories continues to give Ellertsdóttir a deep sense of purpose in her work as a diplomat. She says that women are especially vital around the table in discussions of peace and security issues. Without the opportunity to be at the table, women cannot impact critical problems.

In August 2019, Ellertsdóttir arrived to Washington as Iceland's first woman Ambassador to the U.S. "Look at Washington," she says. "Out of more than 175 diplomatic missions, women represent fewer than thirty. That's not a lot."

One of Ellertsdóttir's colleagues at the Embassy is a thirty-seven-year-old woman. Though the Ministry is split in terms of gender, her colleague shares that she has never contemplated her identity as a women in diplomacy as it seems like a natural occupation for women. "I find it great that more young women don't see as many obstacles," she emphasizes.

In mentoring young women, Ellertsdóttir highlights the importance of curiosity and the pursuit of fulfilling work. "Don't do something just for some stepping stone in your career," she advises. "Do something you like to do, be passionate, be good at it, and that will bring you forward," she says.

She believes until society reaches gender parity, we need to continue talking about women's issues, the importance of women being at the table, women in leadership, and women role models.

To truly make an impact, Ellertsdóttir recommends being good at your job and getting noticed rather than engaging in the "political dance." While the political dance can sometimes pay off, politicians come and go, and the respect earned from colleagues will follow you throughout your career.

Toward the end of our conversation, Ellertsdóttir shares something that she continually carries with her, both professionally and personally. Her parents taught her to respect all people. She says, "It's so fundamental and it sounds kind of simple. But, no matter if it's an ambassador, the IT guy, or the person cleaning your office, show everyone respect, get to know them, [and] appreciate them."

She emphasizes, "In diplomacy, you are meeting many people from different cultures and experiences. You should approach everyone with the same level of respect." Ellertsdóttir attributes this lesson to her parents, claiming, "It's a lesson I received from my parents and I always carry with me. It has made all the difference."

Ellertsdóttir and her nation offer key examples of how opportunity can build impact.

* * *

One institution impacting gender parity is the Organization for Security and Co-operation (OSCE). In Europe, it serves as the largest regional security-focused intergovernmental organization. The OSCE released a sixty-seven-page toolkit in December 2019 entitled "Inclusion of Women and Effective Peace Processes." In the forward of the document, OSCE Secretary General Thomas Greminger addresses why practical guidance is necessary to address the lack of women in the negotiation process:[78]

---

78 Leena Avonius, Meeri-Maria Jaarva, Ulrike Schmidt, and Talia Wohl, "Inclusion of Women and Effective Peace Processes: A Toolkit," Organization for Security and Co-operation in Europe (OSCE), accessed January 12, 2020.

1. Women are differently embedded in society than men are, and they have been shown to widen the range of central topics discussed at the negotiation table.

2. Further inclusive processes can contribute to more comprehensive agreements that better integrate and reflect the concerns of broader society.

3. Ensuring gender diversity in negotiation processes can strengthen the sustainability of the agreements.

Reading through the toolkit provided practical ways stakeholders can address the disparity in the inclusion of women before, during, and after conflict situations globally. (If the toolkit was an Uber driver, I would rate it five stars.)

I originally read about the toolkit from a social media post by Ambassador Melanne Verveer, the first U.S. Ambassador for Global Women's Issues. While attending international relations events, I discussed that I was writing a book focused on gender and diplomacy and I kept hearing the same recommendation for who to interview next: "You have to talk to Melanne Verveer." I connected with her through LinkedIn and began engaging with her posts. One of my contacts generously shared her direct contact information with me, and we set up an in-person interview.

Verveer currently works out of a historic house owned by Georgetown University where she heads the Institute for Women, Peace, and Security. The house blends in with the other historic homes on the street. However, when I enter, it quickly transforms into an organized office with a reception area and Verveer's private space in a large room towards the back. Sunlight streams in through her office windows, highlighting trailing plants, numerous glass awards, and special items collected from her travels. Although she is busily jumping from phone call to phone call behind her desk, I immediately notice her welcoming demeanor. She walks efficiently to a chair and sits near the elegant fireplace with red suede shoes and a navy suit. Verveer has a dignified and compassionate presence.

Verveer has a B.S. and M.S. from Georgetown University and holds several honorary degrees. She is a member of the Council on Foreign Relations and the Trilateral Commission, and she serves on the Boards of the National Endowment for Democracy, the Atlantic Council, and the World Bank Advisory Council on Gender and Development. She is the recipient of numerous awards, including the Secretary of State's Award for Distinguished Service. In 2008, the President of Ukraine awarded her the Order of Princess Olga.

Before her tremendous work on global women's issues, the majority of her career focused on promoting civil rights as the executive director of a progressive advocacy group. Earlier, she served as a Capitol Hill staff member. At that time, she had no idea where her career would ultimately take her.

In a pivotal moment in her professional journey, she served as Chief of Staff to Hillary Clinton in the 1990s. Verveer describes the famous Fourth UN Conference on Women in Beijing that took place in September 1995. In deliberating whether Clinton should attend, Verveer's team weighed competing political perspectives and ideological viewpoints. From the left, they heard that Clinton should not go because it would be putting "a feather in the cap of our archenemy, China, due to human rights violations." From the right, "She shouldn't go because, somehow, this conference was going to destroy the family."

The team determined that the conference was critical and recommended that the First Lady travel to China. Wearing a light pink suit with gold jewelry, Clinton stood up to address the conference comprised of nearly 180 countries. The team understood how much pressure was riding on the words that Clinton was about to utter from the podium. "Human rights are women's rights . . .and women's rights are human rights," echoed in the cavernous room. Her words "catalyzed the women's movement" for that decade.

Clinton listed a litany of human rights abuses that women have endured. During each one she stated, "It is a violation of human rights." The slight translation delay muted the audience's initial response to the address, contributing to Verveer's anxiety about how the speech was being received.

However, Verveer recounts, "You could feel the energy in the room and by the time she finished, the place had erupted in this huge crescendo of applause in reaction to what was said. It was life-changing for me in many ways because, after that, much of the effort that has taken over my life had to do with women's rights as human rights." The year 2020 marks the twenty-fifth anniversary of the conference and the UN General Assembly plans to hold a one-day meeting to commemorate the historic occasion.

From 2000 to 2008, Verveer co-founded Vital Voices Global Partnership to invest in emerging women leaders. She is the co-author of the book *Fast Forward: How Women Can Achieve Power and Purpose.* She also led the effort to establish the President's Interagency Council on Women and was instrumental in the adoption of the Trafficking Victims Protection Act of 2000.

Since 2009, work travel has consumed Verveer's life. In addition to serving in her role at Georgetown University, she also holds the position of Special Representative on Gender Issues for the OSCE Chairmanship. Verveer helps participating countries to implement and execute actions to further gender equality and women's rights.

President Obama and Secretary of State Hillary Clinton initiated the position of U.S. Ambassador for Global Women's Issues to promote women's perspectives and participation in the State Department's policy making and national security work. In this role, Verveer traveled to sixty countries and served as the U.S. Representative to the UN Commission on the Status of Women.

Early in her tenure as the first U.S. Ambassador for Global Women's Issues, the Senate Foreign Relations Committee requested that she testify about the Democratic Republic of Congo (DCR) and the "massive toll on women in terms of sexual violence and how the conflict used rape as a tool of war." In preparation, Verveer asked for a meeting with State Department colleagues who worked on the topic.

Around the conference table at the meeting, a young male desk officer for the DCR asked, "I don't understand what women have to do with any of this?" Verveer was shocked at this disconnect between the Senate's objective of protecting women and this State Department officer's narrow mindset and said to herself, "Obviously, this is going to be harder than I thought it might be."

"It was clear that the work to integrate women into our foreign policy mattered," she states. Verveer understood that her role could help build a consensus to protect women, especially in vulnerable areas. Because of that experience and others, Verveer ensured the issue of gender was central to the State Department's mission, a decision from which "so much work emanated over the years."

She recalls another moment of coalition-building that occurred while working on the Food Security Act, a major initiative of President Obama. A cross-functional team of employees from the State Department and the United States Agency for International Development (USAID) recognized that combatting hunger could also enhance productivity around the world.

Verveer describes the situation. "We were sitting around the table hammering out what should be in the bill, what the indicators might be, and how it was going to be evaluated. We were including all kinds of issues when making this major proposal and gender had not come up."

She looked around the table and noticed that "only a few women were seated among the huge mob." The small group of women asked about women's roles in farming, and it became clear that the majority of small farmers in many countries were women. According to the World Economic Forum, "Studies show that women account for nearly half of the world's smallholder farmers and produce 70 percent of Africa's food. However, less than 20 percent of farm land in the world is owned by women."[79] Verveer thought, "How could you not factor their needs into it?"

To address this disparity, the team decided to incorporate children's nutrition levels and the growth of women's incomes as key indicators of the program's efficacy. Verveer mentions, "It was fortunate the issue came up due to a small number of diverse voices around the table." However, had women's voices not been at the table, the issues most likely would not have been part of the final plan.

She faced a similar situation while working on matters surrounding Afghanistan. One night while Verveer was in Kabul, a group of women she didn't know started a conversation with her. One woman looked Verveer in the eyes and courageously declared out of frustration, "Stop looking at us as victims. Look at us as the leaders that we are." That moment stuck with Verveer, and she explains, "Yes, they have been victimized, some of them terribly, but we are only seeing them through that lens. We are not seeing them in terms of their potential, experience, education, and leadership."

---

79 Jamila Abass, "Women Grow 70% of Africa's Food. But Have Few Rights Over the Land They Tend," World Economic Forum, March 21, 2018.

When she traveled back to the State Department, she understood the necessity of having diversity in discussions of Afghan policy. Afghan women needed to be able to share their experiences on these issues so that they could be factored into the policies and programs that were being developed. Women inside and outside the State Department were vital in "raising the issue of Afghan women." They understood that the role of Afghan women in decision-making was crucial for eventual peace and stability. "Had there not been women voices or validation from the woman Secretary of State, who knows what the policies would have looked like!" remarks Verveer.

While in her State Department role, a group of officials including Verveer met with newly assigned U.S. ambassadors before they left for their posts. She always emphasized, "One of the greatest powers you have is convening power." The group frequently looked at her not able to comprehend how impactful their convening power could be.

During their posts, she heard back from numerous ambassadors. They shared, "You're so right. It's true. When I open the Embassy, I can bring people in for any topic, have discussions, and convene parties who might not typically sit at the table together. They will come to the invitation since I'm the U.S. Ambassador." Through Verveer's words, these ambassadors found they had the power to build coalitions and consensus to "advance more collegial solutions that had seemed evasive or impossible."

In her current role leading the Institute for Women, Peace, and Security at Georgetown University, Verveer addresses the issue of why the roles of women aren't factored into "peace negotiations, reconstruction in post conflicts, and considerations for conflict prevention."

The United Nations Institute for Disarmament Research (UNIDIR) describes the potential harm of this lack of representation. "Diversifying the voices that contribute to decision making can increase effectiveness in problem solving." There are also correlations between women's participation in peace negotiations and conflict meditation with the durability of a peace agreement and the inclusion of gender provisions in the agreements.[80]

Verveer notes, "If you're a diplomat and want to succeed in your work to end conflict in a way that it doesn't reoccur, you need to ensure you've got the best people at the table that can influence the decision." Verveer comments that focusing on gender, in many ways, "goes against the grain of how things were done." She teaches colleagues why including the topic of gender is "both the right thing to do and the smart thing in terms of our overall mission." Explicitly focusing on gender can improve consensus and outcomes.

Throughout her work, Verveer has tried to champion progress without dictating or mandating solutions to colleagues or stakeholders. Instead, she asks two questions:

---

80 Renata Hessmann Dalaqua, Kjølv Egeland, and Torbjørn Graff Hugo, "Still Behind the Curve: Gender Balance in Arms Control, Non-Proliferation and Disarmament Diplomacy," The United Nations Institute for Disarmament Research (UNIDIR), 2019.

1. How can I help you?

2. What do you want to achieve and how can I contribute to that achievement?

Verveer smiles, "It's the old story that everybody has potential, but they don't have the opportunity. When you can match an opportunity with so many people who want to change their lives and help change the lives of others, you really can have a tremendous impact."

PART 4

BALANCE: PERSONAL VS. PROFESSIONAL LIFE

CHAPTER 13

TOUGH DECISIONS

---

*"You should never let your fears prevent
you from doing what you know is right."*

—AUNG SAN SUU KYI

FIRST STATE COUNSELLOR OF MYANMAR AND FIRST
WOMAN TO SERVE AS MINISTER FOR FOREIGN AFFAIRS

Balancing a personal and professional life is challenging. Traveling to a different country or living abroad adds another layer of complexity. Serving your country and remembering its values during difficult situations is an important aspect of being a diplomat, and, in times of stress or war, diplomats can be under immense pressure. They must work to uphold their ideals while no one is watching while facing the reality that their actions can become public at any time. In Washington, many of us followed the initial 2019 impeachment hearings as diplomats took the stand to testify about actions in Ukraine.

While all humans face internal pressure, I have seen firsthand how women tend to internalize stress with perseverance and resilience. Acknowledging this fact and purposely seeking solutions could help provide a more diverse set of voices in public service.

* * *

Aggie Kuperman served as Senior Foreign Service Officer in Iran, Pakistan, Tunisia, Romania, and Germany for the U.S. Department of State. She was a White House Spokesperson for Bosnia, a press officer for the Macedonian peace process, and a public affairs officer in Kabul. Kuperman is a petite woman with cherry red hair, and her elegant voice echoes from a bygone era like a tea that has seeped dark over time.

She lost most of her family while fleeing to the United States from Hungary as a Jewish refugee during the Holocaust. When she and her mother arrived, they had no money and few possessions.

In 1978, Kuperman received her first diplomatic post in Iran through the United States Information Agency. She recalls being around a very large table with twenty people, only two of whom were women. While it seemed that the other woman was slightly hostile to the competition of another woman, the men welcomed her into the circle.

Kuperman served as the Director of the Cultural Center. She recalls, "In Iran, my staff were like an island of peace in the middle of the Revolution. The Cultural Center remained open. Then one day, some Revolutionary Guards came in. They wanted to look at everything."

Kuperman, an avid learner, had picked up Farsi on her own. She loved the language and was able to calmly speak to the Revolutionary Guards, welcoming them to open anything and everything. They looked at her with surprise because they couldn't believe that someone of her gender, age, and stature could be a Director.

She reassured them, smiled calmly, and said, "Yes, I'm the Director. We have nothing to hide here. It's a very nice place. You are welcome to sit down and look at anything, but please don't make a mess because my bosses are very harsh with me. Since I'm relatively new, I don't want to cause any problems for them." The Revolutionary Guards laughed and eventually left without looking through anything.

Her staff was awed by her calm authority and handling of the situation. Kuperman expresses how she was able to face the threat of violence from armed Revolutionary Guards. "Go ahead. Just don't cause me any problems with my bosses." The Cultural Center remained open under Kuperman's leadership until she had to leave her post once the situation in Iran intensified.

Kuperman's ability to respond under pressure is shared by many women. Researcher Dr. Alex Krumer shared in the *Harvard Business Review*, "If you look at the literature on cortisol, the stress hormone, you'll find that levels of it increase more rapidly in men than in women—in scenarios from golf rounds to public speaking—and that those spikes can hurt performance."[81]

Kuperman reflects, "If I were to summarize my life, I think it's an amazing thing that a little immigrant girl with not a penny to her name who lost all her family in the Holocaust was able to become a senior ranking diplomat representing the United States." It's an honor she continues to carry with her.

* * *

As detailed in Part 1, Ambassador Barbara Bodine provides numerous examples of how relationship building is essential for positive diplomatic outcomes, whether in a high-stakes security situation or the day-to-day grind of understanding a region. Her strength as a relationship builder earned her the U.S. Secretary's Award for Valor for her work in Occupied Kuwait. Hers is truly a story worth sharing.

From 1991 through 1994, Bodine was the Associate Coordinator for Operations and overall Coordinator for Counterterrorism at the Department of State. She went on to serve as U.S. Ambassador to Yemen from 1997 to 2001, and in 2003, she was the senior State Department official in Iraq as the Coordinator for Post-Conflict Reconstruction for Baghdad and the Central Regions of Iraq.

---

81   Alison Beard, "Women Respond Better Than Men to Competitive Pressure," *Harvard Business Review*, November-December 2017.

She tells me that she isn't big on victimology or blaming others. Bodine believes you should look to your own agency and inner strength to figure out how and what to do. It was through this method of looking inside herself that she was able to make heart-wrenching decisions as U.S. Deputy Chief of Mission in Kuwait during the Iraqi invasion and occupation of 1990-1991. *Newsweek* published a telling article in 1991 titled "Kuwait: A Rape of Nation."[82] The article is truly not for the faint of heart with the vivid descriptions of rape, torture, and murder.

During her five months in Iraqi-occupied Kuwait, she made an enormous number of extraordinarily difficult decisions. Far from the typical small bureaucratic issues, these decisions were life or death for the people involved. Bodine describes them bluntly as "no shit, oh my G-d, issues." She was responsible for lives, and she understood her country and her soul would hold her accountable if those lives were lost. When Washington headquarters told her she couldn't do something, her response was along the lines of, "Are you going to put me some other place that's awful?" with a tinge of humor and sarcasm.

"I'm sitting here in Kuwait in the middle of an Iraqi invasion, it doesn't get worse than this." She couldn't be threatened and her isolation from the Washington power structure forced her to make decisions on the ground without permission. In her mind, if she ever got back to Washington, she might have to explain the decisions she made, but she felt she had to rely on her instincts to find solutions that would work during the invasion and occupation.

---

82   "Kuwait: Rape of a Nation," *Newsweek*, March 10, 1991.

She came up with some rules of thumb during her time in Kuwait. She asked herself three questions:

1. When do you follow the rules?

2. When do you break them?

3. What do you do when there are no rules?

She elaborates that while diplomats are held accountable for their work, they often find themselves in situations "where the rules simply don't apply and don't even exist." They are tasked with representing their country and being responsible for their decisions. She humbly explains, "You have to be able to live with it, and with yourself, and be able to explain it when you get out." In life and especially diplomacy, Bodine has been forced to bear these many consequences.

During the first two weeks of the invasion of Kuwait, the U.S. Embassy brought Americans—consisting mainly of Embassy staff and families—to their six-acre compound for safety. Bodine recalls roughly three thousand additional American citizens in the city that the Embassy was responsible for as well. In a time before wide adoption of cell phones or the internet, communication was more difficult, and Americans living in the city were in significant danger as potential human shields for invading Iraqis.

Bodine was responsible for this high-stakes game of deciding—based on very limited information—when and how to tell a cohort of Americans to get in their cars and drive to the Embassy. If she guessed wrong, Americans would be driving straight into the hands of the Iraqis. The pressure was immense and she can still feel it to this day. She shares that each time she tells this story, she gets a knot in her stomach. One family in particular still sticks in her memory. The parents were willing to stay behind but they wanted their sixteen-year-old daughter safely out of the country on a convoy. They feared Iraqi troops would take advantage of her.

In a *New Republic* article from March 1991, writer Michael Kelly interviewed a doctor who saw numerous cases of men and women who were "often raped and mutilated before death," in addition to those who were raped and tortured but survived. He described the dismal atmosphere with statistics. "The Iraqis are estimated to have taken as many as twenty thousand prisoners to Iraq to serve as slave laborers and another three thousand to five thousand as hostages and shields in the days just before the allied ground offensive."[83]

In the case of the sixteen-year-old, Bodine was forced to weigh her options. She could put her on a convoy with 140 Americans, but if the Iraqis took over the convoy, she couldn't guarantee the young woman's safety. If she didn't put her on the convoy, and the Iraqis invaded the compound where the family was staying, the young woman could also be in grave danger. Whatever decision she made under this immense pressure, Bodine understood, she would be responsible for the consequences.

---

83 Michael Kelly, "The Rape and Rescue of Kuwaiti City: Torture Victims and Tense Victors," *The New Republic*, March 24, 1991.

She chose to put the three private American citizens, including the sixteen-year-old, on the convoy without telling her superiors. She sat nervously in Kuwait waiting to hear if the convoy made it safely to Turkey. She eventually received a phone call from a colleague in Washington with good news: the convoy had made it. However, her friend also mentioned that there were three people on that convoy that Washington didn't know about and asked Bodine to explain.

She spoke to the Washington colleague on the phone, "Look, if I had told you, then you would have had to tell the Secretary of State and then somebody would have checked with the legal department and then somebody else would have checked with somebody else, and then at some point, somebody would have blabbed it to the press." Ultimately, this would have led to a news story that compromised the safety of these three people and the entire mission.

Bodine explains that if she had told her colleague in Washington, she would have put them in an untenable position of either not being able to share the information or potentially compromising the plan. If she kept the plan to herself, however, it would provide her colleague with plausible deniability. Then, if something went wrong, only Bodine would be responsible. Her colleague questioned this and other risks that she was taking, but Bodine didn't back down and made more decisions like this one during the five month occupation. "Every time I made one of those decisions, I knew that if it didn't work out," Bodine pauses and slowly continues, "it was my responsibility."

According to Bodine, diplomacy requires a willingness to make difficult decisions as opposed to the easy ones. She acknowledges that there will always be people who will second guess those conclusions, but Bodine also shares that the diplomatic community in Kuwait rallied together to support these decisions and bring as many people as possible to safety.

She remembers one circumstance in which a group of twelve Americans was near the Japanese Embassy and couldn't get to the American compound. She called her Japanese colleague on a landline and quickly shared her concern about this group of Americans that the Iraqis were looking for. She started to say that she couldn't get them to the American Embassy, but before she could finish explaining, he said, "Have them come to my Embassy. Get them over here and we will put them in the basement." He did not check with Tokyo—he simply made the high-pressure decision on his own. Multiple embassies took similar actions in Kuwait, protecting lives until the people could make it to their own country's compound.

Bodine recalls another instance when the French evacuated and took four Americans with them. The Canadians called her and said they remembered Tehran during the Iranian Revolution, and they welcomed Americans that needed to come to their Embassy for safety. "Please let them know that the Canadian door is open," the leadership declared. The American Embassy had the same protocol.

Across Kuwait, the diplomatic community protected each other. They understood that although each country had systems, processes, and procedures from their home offices, a full-scale war was underway, and they had to make the right decisions in the moment.

Bodine teaches that, in diplomacy, "there are times when you check, and there are times when you do what is necessary, and then you have to be prepared to answer for it later." Looking back, her decisions saved many lives including that of a sixteen-year-old woman, who later attended UCLA Medical School and became a doctor. As our intense conversation approaches its end, I get tears in my eyes as she finishes her stories about this gut-wrenching time in Kuwait. Saving lives made all this pressure worthwhile.

* * *

War and conflict can bring out the best and worst of humanity. The occupied quickly become the occupier. The secluded minority can become the majority who overrules established norms and society. The meaning of fighting for freedom varies based on who is fighting. The goal of diplomacy is to not go to war; it's to avert it. But if war happens, the goal of diplomacy becomes rebuilding relationships and enabling peaceful resolutions.

The country of Afghanistan has been in search of such resolution for decades. Soviet troops invaded in 1979, initiating almost a decade of fighting with the Mujahideen rebel fighters. According to *The Atlantic*, "An estimated one million civilians were killed, as well as 90,000 Mujahideen fighters, 18,000 Afghan troops, and 14,500 Soviet soldiers."[84] After the Soviet troops rolled their tanks back to the border, a civil war began. In the 1990s, the notorious fundamentalist group called the Taliban took over. Their restrictive presence dominated news reports, depicting brutal gender discrimination under the strict imposition of Sharia law.

For one Afghan, Roya Rahmani, conflict was all she knew; given her nation's tumultuous recent history, no one could have predicted Rahmani's future. Almost four decades after the Soviet invasion, Rahmani, a daughter from a middle-class family in Kabul, would represent Afghanistan as the first woman Ambassador to the United States.

Our interview is rescheduled a few times amidst the news of the Taliban being invited and disinvited to Camp David for negotiations, Afghan elections, the U.S. declaring a potential troop withdrawal from Afghanistan, and attacks by suicide bombers in her country. In other words, Ambassador Rahmani is slightly busy.

Though I don't get the opportunity to meet her in person due to her hectic schedule, I'm enormously appreciative to her and her staff for making a phone call happen. In preparation, I read articles where she is quoted, looked at photos, and watched videos of her speaking. With her loose-fitting hijab gracefully framing her face, her wide eyes show purpose and direction. Her lips are typically painted in shades of red or pink, pursed into a smile.

---

84 Alan Taylor, "The Soviet War in Afghanistan, 1979 - 1989," The
    Atlantic, August 4, 2014.

While speaking on the phone, her smooth voice reminds me of another era similar of women's voices, perhaps of black and white films of the 1930s. Maybe it was the phone, maybe it was the tone of her voice—nonetheless, her quick wit and intellectual prowess vibrate in the air.

After being pushed out of their home, Rahmani tells me how her family fled to Pakistan along with many Afghans escaping the conflict. Her journey eventually led her west where she attended McGill University in Canada. She returned to her home country after graduation in 2004 to work with nonprofit organizations focused on women's education and human rights. She attended Columbia University for a master's degree in Public Administration and International Law and became a Fulbright Scholar. The year 2011 marked when Rahmani joined the Afghan government, first in the Ministry of Education and then in the Ministry of Foreign Affairs.

As part of a team of three, Rahmani was an architect of the Heart of Asia - Istanbul Process initiative. In November 2011, The Heart of Asia established a platform to discuss regional issues, principally security, political, and economic cooperation between Afghanistan and its neighbors. The process recognized that a secure and stable Afghanistan would be the center of prosperity in the region. To date, the Heart of Asia involves fifteen participating countries, seventeen supporting countries, and twelve supporting regional and international organizations. The initiative also led to the establishment of the Director-General for Regional Cooperation position.

The Ministry recognized Rahmani's talent and appointed her as the first Director-General. She served in that role from

2012 to 2016 and led the Afghanistan representation, including more than a dozen regional organizations. It was the first time Afghanistan held a leadership role in a project directly impacting its country and region. Rahmani found herself to be the only woman in the room on numerous occasions.

As male colleagues would enter the room and see her at the head of the table, the senior men would question whether they were in the right place. In part-statement-part-question, they would ask, "We have her as chair of this negotiation?" As a younger woman, Rahmani broke stereotypes just by being in the room, let alone in leading the discussion.

The United Nations Institute for Disarmament Research (UNIDIR) notes, "Women are frequently underrepresented in international forums concerned with peace and security, and targeted actions to improve women's participation are required."[85] Rahmani encountered considerable pushback, usually in the form of patronizing language and facial expressions. She recalls chairing a counterterrorism meeting in which she would enter the room and the men would "not greet or take notice of her." According to the OSCE, "Women in negotiating delegations, particularly younger ones, tend to be closely scrutinized and even belittled by their older male counterparts. At times, women negotiators are ignored when speaking. At others, gendered language is used to attack them."[86]

---

85 "Gender & Disarmament Resource Pack for Multilateral Practitioners," The United Nations Institute for Disarmament Research (UNIDIR), January 2019.

86 Leena Avonius, Meeri-Maria Jaarva, Ulrike Schmidt, and Talia Wohl, "Inclusion of Women and Effective Peace Processes: A Toolkit," Organization for Security and Co-operation in Europe (OSCE), accessed January 12, 2020.

Year by year, Rahmani says, this slowly changed. Eventually, people would approach her and say, "In the beginning, we were doubtful of you, but you proved yourself and we're happy you're doing it." However, as capital cities around the world sent different negotiators, the process would begin again. Prove oneself, rinse, repeat.

Rahmani tells me that throughout her diplomatic career, she has encountered people who have tried to work against her. "For me, the biggest question was, why would people go out of their way to make something difficult for somebody else? What is it that they get [out of it]?"

Rahmani says she doesn't experience envy—it's not even part of her lexicon. Rahmani works with what she calls "full passion." If she doesn't feel passionate about what she is doing, she is unable to do it. In her diplomatic work, she's learned that she dives in with focus and personally cares about the outcome. However, if senior leadership is not invested or has a different political motivation, this passion "go[es] down the drain."

Rahmani firmly believes, "the truth will prevail when your intentions are good and when what you want to do is good. There is always backstabbing, accusations, lying—a whole range of things to get to the point of intimidation. But people will come around."

She remembers a group of people that would joke about her. After multiple encounters, these same people wanted Rahmani's attention. "They would say hello and salute out of respect. It took a lot of time and patience. I just continued doing what I needed to do."

Rahmani feels that there should always be a calculus. If you do something, what do you get out of it? She explains that it doesn't have to be something physical and can be as simple as fulfillment or joy. "It doesn't add up to make something difficult for somebody else or if you benefit and take joy from people in anguish," she notes. She divulges to me that the intensity of the war in Afghanistan and the suffering of the children keeps her awake at night.

After her role as Director-General, Rahmani served as Afghanistan's Ambassador to Indonesia and the Association of Southeast Asian Nations. Rahmani strongly believes that if she wants to do something, she can. She enjoys the challenge of pouring herself into her work, but she doesn't want it to be a waste. She knows that many people around the world must wonder if her efforts will be a waste due to Afghanistan's turbulent relationship with the Taliban.

In a December 2019 interview with *The Washington Diplomat*, Rahmani says, "They cannot push young women back inside their houses, they cannot ask young boys to give up their hopes and surrender to the kind of ideologies they were perpetuating. The recent election was a very clear example of our resolve. Under gunpoint—literally, because the Taliban had declared a war on our election—the people of Afghanistan took the time to register, find their polling stations, and vote.

We are demonstrating our commitment to democracy, and I hope our partners do the same."[87]

As the Ambassador of Afghanistan to the U.S., Rahmani is often asked, "How do you like living in Washington?" She answers by saying, "I cherish it and it's a privilege." She says she doesn't want to lose sight of the "huge responsibility" of being posted in Washington. This one city is pivotal as the location of crucial decision making on a daily basis. Government officials write reports, present data, and create statements that "impact the lives of people they never knew and will never know."

The choices made in Washington, Brussels, New York, or Geneva often impact human beings that will never set foot in those cities. But people are complex. Our wants, desires, emotions, and thoughts swirl within us. We are neither all good nor all bad.

Challenges and tough decisions fuel Rahmani's fire. Her mantra is "very simple—quitting is not an option. That's it." At the time this book is written, Rahmani is only one of four Afghan women to serve as ambassadors. Their participation is part of the 20 percent of women serving in Afghanistan's Foreign Ministry.

Toward the end of our interview, Rahmani poignantly says, "Everything, at the end of the day, is personal. We should not lose sight of the fact that this world is run by human

---

87   Larry Luxner, "Afghanistan's First Female Ambassador to U.S. Insists Peace Is Still Possible," *The Washington Diplomat*, December 3, 2019.

beings. Human beings with feelings, human beings with ego, human beings with kindness, human beings with envy, and everything that makes a human being. Nothing is absolute and everything is personal."

Silence fills the air as I meditate on her poetic words. She then asks, "Are you there?"

It's at this moment that I realize how imperative it is to have women like Rahmani as advocates, determining the future of complex conflicts. While tough decisions are being made for and by her country, the knowledge that diplomats like Rahmani have a seat at the table keeps me hopeful.

CHAPTER 14

ACHIEVING A CAREER AND FAMILY

———

*"I am my own woman . . . and was, long before
I became Prime Minister. Attending to my
family's needs only made me stronger as a leader
because if you know how to run a home and
ensure each person's particular need is met, it's
the best leadership training you can have."*

—KAMLA PERSAD-BISSESSAR

FIRST WOMAN PRIME MINISTER OF
TRINIDAD AND TOBAGO

In my research, I sit down with women who work at NGOs, think tanks, and organizations on the periphery of diplomacy. I ask them, "What are you most curious about? What do you want to learn from leaders in diplomacy?" One resounding theme emerges: balancing a career and family life *and* insider advice on how to grow your career. "How do they do it?"

a few friends of mine ask. They want to understand how women leaders can rise to the top of their field while having children and a family.

My interviews reveal that there isn't a holy grail of work-life balance, but rather multiple ways in which women balance their lives. Some women are single, some are married with no children, some *are* married with children, and some are divorced. While their personal lives are not part of the central questions I ask during the interviews, the strength and support of a family seems to have benefitted their careers.

Mexican Ambassador Martha Bárcena notes that balance consists of maintaining your identity, family, and connection to your country. As she puts it, you need time to focus on yourself, your family, and your home country. For twelve years, Bárcena saw her husband, another career diplomat, only on the weekends.

She recalls "serving in Denmark while he was serving in Finland, [and] when I was serving in Turkey he was serving in Romania." They were the first couple in the Mexican Foreign Service to become ambassadors at the same time. She reveals to me that her children "knew they could always count on their parents" even while living abroad.

Before social media and smart phones, Bárcena tells me about how she would write letters and set fixed times each Sunday to call family members. Today's technology makes it much easier to be connected and "constantly distracted." She jokes that, "If every foreign minister or ambassador constantly tweets, in the end, people won't pay attention anymore." Technology has its role, and using it to connect to family while abroad can be very helpful. As we discuss how technology connects Bárcena to her family, she enthusiastically shows me photos of her grandchild on her phone.

As for the unmarried women I interview, they remain connected to their parents or siblings for support. Some of them wish they were dating, but finding a partner while building a transient career is challenging. Some diplomats elect to build their families before entering the foreign service, while others meet their partner overseas. Whichever form a family takes, it is frequently the backbone of support for diplomats.

At the risk of stating the obvious, everyone benefits from having a personal team, crew, group, or "posse" of people who understand them and whom they can trust. At the same time, moving every few years is simultaneously an exciting adventure and a drain on families, depending on one's perspective. What I find most moving are the stories of women diplomats trusting their gut to tell them when to put aside or focus on their career. Women everywhere are constantly trying to find balance.

Austrian Ambassador Eva Nowotny—introduced in Chapter 4—is thankful to have been lucky in both her professional and personal life. She had three consecutive ambassadorial postings in Paris, London, and Washington, and ended up marrying another foreign service officer. Upon arriving in London, she was the first woman Ambassador to bring her husband. To her surprise, this led to questions of protocol for the British. Who would sit where? What events would her spouse be invited to? Her posting helped lay the groundwork for future women ambassadors bringing spouses.

Nowotny is thankful that she and her partner "could develop their careers in parallel." They were posted together and shared a personal life that grounded and supported them in their respective careers. They took turns growing professionally.

Nowotny recognizes, "It is an issue for women in diplomacy that sometimes it isn't easy for them to adjust their personal life and their private life." A foreign service career involves constant relocation, and a diplomat's house, life, and partner must be flexible. However, Nowotny says, "It's usually very difficult on partnerships." While the foreign service offers fascinating career opportunities, it is a very challenging field for adjusting and maintaining one's personal life.

Nowotny feels strongly that "It's always helpful to have a partner, because it's not easy adapting to life in a different country under completely different circumstances with many special demands." A diplomat's professional life has many social obligations. In addition to managing an embassy, ambassadors manage a residence and household and must frequently entertain on behalf of their country. Because of this, Nowotny says, "It's very important to have a reliable partner who supports you and keeps you down to earth, because it's a profession where it's easy to lose the ground under your feet."

A romantic partnership can strengthen a diplomat's support system. But what happens when children are brought into the mix? Countries are still figuring out where to place that puzzle piece. But Sweden seems to be closer than most.

During my visit to the Swedish Embassy to interview Ambassador Karin Olofsdotter, her press secretary gives me a quick tour after the discussion. In the basement of the Embassy's modern glass building near an inside water pond, doors opened to a dark room. Life-size photographs of children being cared for adorn the walls. What makes the photographs stand out? Only dads are depicted with their children.

In these photos, one dad shops for groceries with children in the cart, another vacuums with a child on his back, another bathes a child in a sink with water splashing in the air, another dresses the children, and so on. The photographed fathers stayed home with their children for at least six months of paternity leave. Photographer Johan Bävman's "Swedish Dads" exhibit was purposefully displayed at the Swedish Embassy for U.S. audiences to view, with the hope of encouraging the spread of family-friendly parental paid leave and gender equality in the States.[88] The exhibit is traveling the world to spread the message.

Olofsdotter claims, "If it had been women photographed, it would never even have been an exhibit." When mothers engage in the daily tasks of child-rearing, it's rarely

---

88   Johan Bävman, "Swedish Dads," accessed January 16, 2020.

newsworthy. "We think it is so fantastic because it's men," Olofsdotter notes sarcastically, "but these are things that women have been doing for thousands of years." She believes both parents are needed in a child's life. Fortunately, the Swedish system allows parents to stay home after a child is born for 480 days and receive money from the government. An impressive ninety days of leave are given to each parent no matter what. There's also a bonus given to parents who equitably divide these days.

However, even with this exceptional policy, only 14 percent of Swedish parents choose to share the days equally. Even so, Olofsdotter believes the Swedish policy for parental leave is "extremely important." In the Swedish Ministry of Foreign Affairs, employees receive 90 percent of their wages during their government-sponsored paternal leave. According to Olofsdotter, "A man who does not take at least six months of parental leave is looked upon with suspicion."

It is often the case that men earn more than women and say they cannot stay home because the family would lose too much money. However, with the government-sponsored program and especially in the Foreign Ministry, this argument does not land. The program ensures that it doesn't help or hurt anyone's career to take time off, thus making parental leave a non-issue. More importantly, when considered for promotion in Sweden, neither men nor women are disadvantaged by their amount of parental leave. As a result, this policy helps promote gender equality. While women are still the bearers of children, this parental leave policy makes considerable strides in equalizing the career advancement of men and women foreign service officers.

Another diplomat I talk to touches on a different aspect of domestic life in the foreign service—that women are the ones to pick up the pieces when moving to a different country. Mothers are the ones to ask, what is the education system like in this new post? What kind of activities and culture will the children partake in? To that end, French diplomat Laure Pallez advises future generations of foreign service officers to immerse themselves in the local environment and make an effort to understand a country's culture.

With a quiet disposition, a sharp jawline, and a quick pep in her step, Pallez moves swiftly around the French Embassy in Washington. Her perceptive eyes emphasize her innate ability to instantly read a room, and she exudes a serious, strong, and thoughtful demeanor.

Pallez spent twelve years working and living in China before her posting to Washington as Deputy Economic Counselor. Her career spans from finance to marketing, client management, credit analyst, chief business officer, politics, and now, the foreign service. Pallez is a third-generation public servant and affirms, "My whole family has always been very involved in public service. That's why I have it in my heart to serve my country. It's having the best interest of all people."

Pallez's experience in Asia was a pivotal turning point in her career. The dichotomy of Eastern and Western cultures was extreme, she says, explaining how the Chinese see the long game in a span of generations. This culture was much different than that of her French upbringing, which espouses seizing enjoyment in the moment.

Pallez's time in China shaped her ideas about harmony and a woman's ability to evoke global change. She says that Chinese women seem to have the same upward mobility and opportunities as men. Pallez recalls the famous saying of Mao Zedong that "women hold up half the sky." This mantra has stayed with her throughout her career. She explains that, "It's based on equality between men and women. You see a lot of that in China, where women have interesting positions within the party or an organization, because they represent 'half the sky,' according to common thinking."

Pallez is straightforward in sharing the impressive human and technical abilities of the Chinese women she encountered. "They were never just the wives of someone. In China, women were strong in political careers, strong in technical careers such as scientists, and that inspired me very much."

While in China, Pallez received an opportunity to run for politics alongside a close mentor back in France, but she ultimately decided to accept the post in Washington. Pallez says her two children motivated this decision. Although she shares that her mind is never clear—constantly darting from work to family issues—she believes women have the essential ability to understand the long game of building generations.

She envisions her children's futures in the world of policy and economics. As a mother and a diplomat, Pallez is concerned with creating a better world. She encourages other women by saying, "Don't limit yourself, you *can* do it all. Your kids will be happy to see you happy." In moving her career forward, Pallez understands the nuances of creating harmony at breakneck speed.

* * *

In my multiple interviews, some women diplomats contribute more personal stories. Some ask whether they should share certain information, and others offer it freely. Former Hungarian Ambassador Reka Szemerkényi closes our interview by sharing the ultimate takeaways of her time as Ambassador.

From 2015 to 2017, Szemerkényi devoted her time to creating relationships and building community. I happen to have witnessed her warm and gracious community-building firsthand. During her time as Ambassador, I attended a private Hungarian wine tasting dinner at the Embassy. It was an elegant evening of schmoozing U.S. trade officials and Hungarian winemakers with the aim of the United States importing more Hungarian wine.

Hungary is renowned for its famous Bull's Blood red wine. (It's not blood, but what a great name!) Szemerkényi welcomed guests and stayed the whole evening. Hearty conversations and wine flowed generously over Hungarian culinary pairings. I hazily recall how Szemerkényi's presence created that atmosphere of community. Albeit a community of Bull's Blood wine lovers, but a community nonetheless.

While Szemerkényi traveled around as Ambassador of Hungary to the United States, she met with business leaders, Hungarian-American organizations, and other organizations to forge relationships on behalf of her country. From "California to Boston, Texas to Florida" or wherever she went, she aimed to build communities with heart.

With the utmost sincerity, Szemerkényi shares with me the secret to her success. "You can only be successful professionally if you use your brain to full capacity, but the bravery of adding heart is something that I think makes a difference." According to Szemerkényi, one of the added values of women in diplomacy is the "balance of heart and mind that women bring without knowing it."

Szemerkényi learned this powerful lesson early on, during her travels with the Hungarian prime minister to visit the Hungarian troops running international operations in the Balkans. She was there in her official capacity as State Secretary for Foreign Policy and as the National Security Advisor. However, Szemerkényi recalls seeing the situation through her perspective as a mother. Through this lens, she saw what was at stake. Looking at the soldiers, she saw sons and daughters of other mothers. Szemerkényi understood the serious implications and experienced "a very deep feeling of what [could] be lost" in the use of militaristic force. She calls this "the real stakes."

Szemerkényi visited Hungarian troops in the Balkans and peacekeeping operations in Cyprus and Afghanistan. In these moments, she recalls feeling a special responsibility for the soldiers. These were not just faceless men and women, and the choices of the government and politicians were not just "paper decisions." Szemerkényi recalls, "I felt the full weight and responsibility of the decision making as these soldiers were the country's children."

Speaking candidly, Szemerkényi reaffirms the need for both genders in diplomacy and all decision-making spheres. "A combination of men and women," Szemerkényi explains, "creates a dynamic interaction of thinking from different approaches." Each gender is designed differently and thinks differently, she says, but ultimately needs to cooperate at the table. The first step, Szemerkényi says, is that, "You have to be there."

Over the decades, Szemerkényi has given many speeches. From China and Japan to across the U.S., she has shared her expertise and views on security policy and diplomacy. Looking back, Szemerkényi notices a trend among all types of groups—from universities and professional conferences to policy panels. She remarks, "Most of the men who came up to me after a speech I gave asked questions about the topic from the panel discussion." What surprised Szemerkényi was the recurring question asked by women: "How did you manage to combine a family and professional life?" She describes this concern as "completely global."

This question has led Szemerkényi to understand the "deep desire of women to 'have both.'" She notes that women around the world face this same challenge. She describes her conquest of balance as the feeling that "life is complete when we have both." The balance of working professionally and raising four children has afforded Szemerkényi the heart and intensive perseverance to succeed professionally.

She says that striving for this balance created an eagerness to utilize all her talents, as a diplomat and a mother.

She adds that the pursuit of balancing both inspires her. While she admits it's sometimes a difficult balancing act, the importance of having both afforded her more focus. To Szemerkényi, career and family are of equal importance.

With conviction, Szemerkényi tells other mothers, "Don't give it up. It's definitely doable. It's very hard. It's not an easy way. But don't think it's not possible. Don't think you have to choose. . . . It's not a choice between the two, but a choice of a combination of the two." Szemerkényi says that for both men and women encountering this struggle, balancing both is equally valid and imperative to success.

Szemerkényi also believes that this balance creates harmony in both the family and one's own life. Szemerkényi speaks directly with a calm, Yoda-like presence as she says, "You have to be convinced that you're not taking away from your partner, you're not taking away from your children, but [that] this balance is completing your life." Szemerkényi's wisdom reverberates in my other discussions of this topic.

* * *

Diplomacy is comprised of multiple threads: traditional diplomats, government officials, and advocates who work in the field. Many of us also practice diplomacy in our everyday interactions. Washington is home to many lobbying, advocacy, and strategic communication firms, all of which engage in various iterations of diplomacy. In Washington, K Street is an infamous stretch of road where many of these organizations are headquartered.

I recall a brisk walk along K Street in September, crossing through Farragut Square. I try to hurry but avoid sweating through my clothing, and my walk turns into a jog in heeled wedges. Food trucks line the curb of the street and delicious scents waft through the air, reminding me that I should have eaten lunch. I hustle into the tall office building north of the square, and my adrenaline subsides as my interviewee wraps up a meeting. Good thing, as I need a few moments to settle.

Sally Painter, Co-Founder and Chief Operating Officer at Blue Star Strategies, welcomes me into her bright office. Her work encompasses foreign and security policy guidance, external affairs, and global business development.

Painter served as a lead advisor for global NATO Summits in Washington in 1999, Prague in 2002, Istanbul in 2004, and Riga in 2006. Her work promoting democracy and alliances has touched Albania, Azerbaijan, the Democratic Republic of Congo, Kazakhstan, Romania, Ukraine, Uzbekistan, and more. In researching her many board positions and accomplishments, I find that she is also a recipient of the Golden Laurel Branch Award from Bulgaria, the Officer's Cross of the Order of Merit from Hungary, and the Minister of Defense Award for Distinction from Latvia.

This blue-eyed modern professional sits down in a hip suit jacket and work-appropriate combat boots. *That sure beats wearing heels* crosses my mind as my swollen feet engulf my wedges.

Painter's spunk is immediately energizing while her colleague's dog rests peacefully against the wall. I sit on a fluffy angled couch as Painter says, "For the longest period of my career, I was the only woman and I was definitely the youngest woman."

Painter's mere presence in the room changed the dynamic. Painter landed in Washington around 1980. She wanted to work in politics on Capitol Hill but had no connections, so she started work for a private company. The 1992 presidential election rolled in, and Painter was pregnant. In October, her son was born. Painter was thirty years old. Shortly after, Bill Clinton was elected to the presidency.

Painter recalls overhearing among her Washington crew that an inaugural committee was forming. She thought, "Great! I'm going to volunteer." Painter's goal was to get a ticket to the Inaugural Ball because it was the first president she was sincerely passionate about supporting. She called the inaugural headquarters and they told her to come down to help with the phone bank.

Because she was on maternity leave at the time, Painter secured the nursing part of her body so nothing would leak. With two to three hours before the next feeding, she drove herself down to the Navy Yard neighborhood where a set of "disheveled buildings" had been torn down. She entered a building and approached a little room with about seven chairs. A woman— the gatekeeper of the phone bank—sat up front.

The woman asked Painter, "Why are you here?"

"Oh, I called, and they said they needed people for the phone bank," she replied warmly.

All the chairs were full, so the woman told her to come back later. Painter left for a short time and returned with determination.

Still no open chairs.

She asked the woman again and was further brushed off. Painter waited another fifteen minutes and the woman remarked, "We just don't have any room."

Painter respectfully left the woman's desk and walked around the corner to a hallway. She found a chair, sat down and tried not to sob. Thoughts raced through her mind: "What the hell am I doing here? I don't know anybody. I have a baby at home!"

Her internal dialogue came to a sharp halt as a man approached and asked, "Are you here for the political meeting?" She noticed the door next to her and looked at him. With nothing to lose, she casually replied, "Yeah."

Painter followed the unknown man into the room and sat next to him. Two and a half hours into the meeting, Painter was vigorously volunteering for assignments divvied up around the table. She could also feel her breast milk starting to leak under her black turtleneck and blazer.

Painter remembers listening to the roll call around the table. She was sitting next to Ron Brown, the head of the inaugural committee, along with Madeleine Albright, Rahm Emanuel, and others. "Basically, the senior structure of the Clinton administration," Painter explains. At the time, she didn't know who was "important." She just knew everyone was important, and she was going to be as helpful as possible.

Her job started the next day—her office was next to Brown's. Painter had an underlying fear of someone asking, "Who are you and why are you here?" After working two weeks on the job, the calm, cool, and collected Brown entered her office and slammed the door. The conversation went something like this:

"Who are you?" he demanded quizzically.

In a rapid cry, "My name is Sally Painter and . . ."

"Nobody knows who you are. How did you get in here?"

"Well, you brought me in here."

"I brought you in here?"

"Yeah, you asked me to come into that meeting."

"But everyone acted like they knew you."

"Well yeah, because I came in with you."

Shocked and exasperated, he said, "WHAT? You could've been an ax murderer! You could've been a Republican plant! How did this happen?!"

"I would never lie. I was on maternity leave. And no one ever asked me. So, I took the job."

After an unorthodox start, Painter served as a senior advisor in the Clinton Administration in the office of the Secretary of Commerce Ronald H. Brown from 1993 to 1995. From that experience, she learned that everyone is important, and you must treat every experience like a job interview. After all, anything can end up becoming a job.

"Women have got to stop being self-deprecating and self-conscious. We have to stand up for ourselves and ask," Painter shares.

As January began, her work in the White House picked up full steam. She was traveling frequently, providing advice and advocacy for U.S companies bidding on overseas contracts, and assisting on NATO issues. Her son was only a few months old.

On one of her trips to Latvia, Painter became close friends with Vaira Vīķe-Freiberga, the first woman President of Latvia. Painter mentions this name a few times.

(The last name "Vīķe-Freiberga" is simply fun to say with its sound and cadence. I hope you give it a try by saying it out loud: Vīķe-Freiberga. Thank you, let's continue.)

While conversing after a meeting, Vīķe-Freiberga noticed Painter was agitated. She told Painter, "You're upset because your son is home and he is young. While you're here in Latvia, you're far from him."

Painter responded, "I *am* upset! As much as this is my dream come true . . ."

Before Painter could finish her sentence, Vīķe-Freiberga stopped her. "Sally, let me tell you something. You can have everything. You can have it all. But you can't have it all at the same time."

She continued. "Here's what you do. Bring him with you. Everywhere you go, since you're with the government, you have an Embassy that's putting things together. Call the Embassy in advance, find out who has a child your son's age, and set up playdates. By the time you're done with work for the day, you can still see your son."

Painter followed her guidance. While her son is no longer a young child, he has been to forty countries, met multiple leaders, and has friends around the globe. How mothers blend career and family is a personal choice. But, as Painter's experience illustrates, women have the power to make those choices. Create your priorities. Be determined like Painter, and ask.

"It's not easy. But you don't have to choose motherhood [over] your career," Painter confided.

In her work, especially focused on NATO issues, Painter encountered different women with the same question: *how do we solve it?* rather than, *who's in control?* Painter says that women offer a different viewpoint and diversity enables an authentic perspective.

Towards the end of our conversation, Painter shares the recipe to her secret sauce: hard work, risk, and luck. The third item has a disclaimer. "You make your luck," Painter says.

It wasn't until I left the fast-paced, thirty-minute meeting that I noticed the koi fishpond in the building lobby. How did I not hear the trickling water and see the bright orange fish? I ponder that it's funny how when you rush, you don't notice what is right in front of you.

I stop and gently remind myself to slow down and notice. I take a moment to let my conversation with Sally Painter sink in. Her vivacious and curious spirit. Her sincere appreciation of being a mother and having a career in diplomacy. Her candid demeanor and attitude of tenacity.

I walk back through Farragut Square with a renewed sense of courage and determination.

* * *

I notice a trend in learning about the different global practices for family and career balance. Countries that institute adequate parental leave for both genders tend to have greater diversity in multiple levels of leadership. Parental and family leave are the crux of workplace equality. "Giving paternity leave alongside maternity leave is something that indicates that it is a shared responsibility," said Mohamed Abushahab, UAE Ambassador to Belgium and the EU.[89] The act of both parents taking parental leave helps remove bias from hiring and promoting decisions. For those who do not have children, a balance of personal and professional life is still necessary (and a family leave policy could encompass taking

---

89   Gillian Duncan, "Women are Making Strides in Diplomacy, But Progress is Painfully Slow," *The National*, November 19, 2018.

care of one's parents.) Flexibility is at the center of achieving work-life balance.

The United Nations Institute for Disarmament Research developed a toolkit in 2018 with recommendations on how to foster an inclusive culture.[90] These suggestions aim to propose a work-life balance that helps both men and women. The toolkit recognizes that women "bear more unpaid household and care work than men." To aid in that reality, they suggest instituting family-friendly arrangements, especially for meetings that run over. When "endgame diplomacy" happens and diplomats cannot leave a negotiation, meeting leaders must provide adequate warning.

The World Bank Group's Women, Business and the Law document identifies a significant parallel between childcare support and women's representation in parliaments.[91] Here are two statistics I found fascinating:

1. Government support for early childcare to employers, childcare centers, and parents can increase the likelihood of women's representation in national parliaments by 25 percent or more.

2. With 25 percent or more women representation in parliaments, the likelihood of laws mandating government

---

90 Renata Hessmann Dalaqua, Kjølv Egeland, and Torbjørn Graff Hugo, "Still Behind the Curve: Gender Balance in Arms Control, Non-Proliferation and Disarmament Diplomacy," The United Nations Institute for Disarmament Research (UNIDIR), 2019.

91 "Women, Business and the Law 2016: Getting to Equal," World Bank Group, accessed January 20, 2020.

support to parents, employers, and childcare centers for preschool childcare services for older age groups increases.

To accomplish professional goals and manage one's family, women diplomats need freedom, flexibility, and support. After hearing from these women leaders about the multiple ways in which they balance their lives, I do not see family and career as mutually exclusive. With personal life and a professional life woven together, we can find greater meaning.

CHAPTER 15

EQUILIBRIUM THROUGH DIVERSITY

———

"It's very difficult to evaluate a leader in a very short-term perspective because to be a leader, you must be able to have a long-term perspective. You must be able to carry changes which take many years. And this is why you can really only see whether it has been a good leadership after some years have passed."

— GRO HARLEM BRUNDTLAND
FIRST WOMAN PRIME MINISTER OF
NORWAY AND SERVED THREE TERMS

Equilibrium is something my friends and colleagues constantly strive for. I never feel quite in balance. I try to focus my efforts with razor-sharp precision, but it can feel like I'm juggling many balls—and often dropping some. I don't have any children, but I can imagine how the aspect of family adds many balls to a juggler's hands. As a young child, I learned the mantra of "where there is a will, there is a way," and this has always seemed to help me control the swirling balls I continue to juggle in my life.

On a brisk autumn day, I find myself in juggle-mode, hurriedly rushing to the Australian Embassy. After going through security and a bag check, I wait in the expansive lobby as another Embassy desk calls the executive suite where the offices of the Ambassador and Deputy Head of Mission are located. An elevator ride and two secure doors grant me access to the "executive office suite" where phones are not permitted.

Modern black leather couches, inherited from her predecessor, flank Ambassador Katrina Cooper's private corner office overlooking Massachusetts Avenue. After holding the rank of Ambassador in a previous post, she became the Deputy Head of Mission, also known as the Deputy Chief of Mission, at the Australian Embassy in Washington in October 2017. This is a fairly common arrangement, given the importance of the Washington post. She graciously agrees to move our meeting to a small conference room on another level of the Embassy so I can record our conversation on my phone.

Cooper strides the Embassy halls confidently. She sports cropped blonde hair and a gray jacket with an angled neckline. Silver and gold rings adorn her fingers as she quickly opens doors and takes us to a private room.

Similar to her walk, Cooper has a quick banter. She's a "think fast, talk fast" kind of gal. Before her posting in Washington, she held the esteemed position of Senior Legal Advisor in the Canberra headquarters at the Department of Foreign Affairs and Trade, where she shaped the Women in Leadership initiative. Cooper originally joined the foreign service in 1992, after earning a bachelor of arts and bachelor of law with honors from the Australian National University. She is also an accredited Australian legal practitioner. She served as the Second Secretary in Chile from 1995 to 1998 and then as a Counselor in Papua New Guinea from 2002 to 2005. From 2008 to 2012, Cooper was Australia's first woman Ambassador to Mexico and represented her country in Costa Rica, Cuba, Guatemala, Honduras, Nicaragua, the Dominican Republic, El Salvador, and Panama.

In 2003, Cooper had been in the Department for Foreign Affairs and Trade for a handful of years. She was on maternity leave after giving birth to her second child. Three days after giving birth, she asked her husband to take care of the baby so she could attend an important meeting. Australia was rolling out a significant development assistance package in another country. Cooper knew that she wanted to be at the table even though she had just started her maternity leave. She thought, "If we didn't get it right, it wouldn't work."

Around the long table, the diplomats discussed the implementation of the package. She quickly realized she was the only woman in the room. During the discussions, she intervened in the conversation to encourage parties to think "equally hard" about *how* they would roll out the program. Figuring out the approach and the needed conversations with the partner country were equally critical. For Cooper, "An incredibly important part of diplomacy is relationships."

Silence spread along the table, and everyone looked at her. No one said anything. Then the group picked up the conversation where it had left off almost ignoring her comment.

This pivotal moment stuck with her for three reasons:

1. She asked herself, "Why am I in this room?" With a three-day old baby waiting to breastfeed, what were her priorities?

2. Not being acknowledged gave her a feeling of being alone, especially as the only woman at the table.

3. She realized, "My point was valid so I'm just going to keep making my points."

In 2012, she was finishing her stint as the first woman to serve as Australian Ambassador to Mexico. Cooper and her husband had adopted a young Mexican girl, so she had decided to take a year off to focus on her family. During that year, the Ministry offered her a promotion to Senior Legal Advisor. She said she couldn't take the role at the time because she had already planned the much-needed sabbatical with her family.

Her boss consoled her, "Well, never mind. You're very competitive, so give it a try when the next bulk-hiring for leadership happens."

She paused. "This is why we don't have many women in leadership."

"What do you mean?" he responded.

"It's too hard—you make it too hard. We just have to close our eyes and cross our fingers and hope it all works out because that's all we can do."

He let her know he would ask the current Senior Legal Advisor to delay his retirement so Cooper could take up the role after her sabbatical. It ended up working, but the process bothered her. The promotion process didn't have the flexibility required to both develop her personal life and promote professional growth.

As Cooper began working at this senior level, her supervisor, a Deputy Secretary, said to her, "I want you to always speak up. Don't stop speaking." She understood it was a "good message for all people, but particularly women" because oftentimes, there is a gender disparity among senior leadership. Hearing this recommendation from a senior male leader was "enormously helpful" for Cooper. It showed how allies and leadership play a crucial part in moments of needed encouragement and support.

In the senior-level role, Cooper looked around the leadership table and was "shocked." She recalls asking herself, "Why aren't there more women around the table?" It had been more than twenty years since Cooper had originally joined the foreign service. Her graduating foreign service class had twenty-five people: thirteen women and twelve men. She remembered while in training, an older male diplomat presented the topic about life at a diplomatic post. He kept speaking about what their "wives" might do or how to entertain or help occupy their "wives." One of the women class members spoke up.

"Excuse me, I'm not sure you noticed, but more than half of us in this class are women. Not all of us will have wives."

Afterward, the women of the group laughed and asked their colleague why she was rude to the man. The colleague jabbed, "It's just absurd." Cooper "assumed that everyone was equal and they would all rise equally" in the foreign service. "The gender thing didn't occur to me at all," she shares.

When Cooper gained access to the leadership table and saw fewer women, she was no longer laughing. It wasn't funny anymore. She wondered what had happened and decided, "We need to do something about it." It wasn't part of Cooper's job description, however, so she took some of the lessons she learned from a leadership course at the Harvard Kennedy School and decided to apply them to the situation.

Cooper gathered a group of like-minded people, who had already been thinking about this. She also sought advice from Elizabeth Broderick, a former Australian Sex Discrimination Commissioner, who had been "very effective in her role." Broderick shared her number one ingredient for success with Cooper: get the leader on board.

Cooper spent ten months encouraging discussions of the gender imbalance at senior levels in the Ministry, including with the Secretary of the Department of Foreign Affairs and Trade Peter Varghese. He was "on board with the idea" of finding out why more women weren't making it to senior leadership levels. Originally, he wanted Cooper to be the champion of the project and lead it, but she declined. It was vital that the initiative be led from the top.

Instead, leadership hired a consultant to make an assessment of the organization, review all the processes, and make recommendations based on the discovered reasons why women weren't advancing as quickly as men. From that process, twelve months later, Secretary Varghese announced the Ministry's Women in Leadership Strategy. Cooper was part of the Steering Committee that formulated a plan for implementation of the recommendations. The plan, titled the "Women in Leadership Strategy: Promoting Equality and Dismantling Barriers," proved to be very effective.[92] It even won the Australia Public Service Gender Equality Award for driving deep cultural change in the Ministry. "If you step up and do something and do it in the right way, you can bring the whole organization with you," Cooper explains.

One of the most significant decisions of the plan was to include targets, not quotas.

I inquire about Cooper's thoughts of targets versus quotas for gender equality. "Targets are aspirational," she notes. When working on the plan, there was a large discussion "around merit." The Department of Foreign Affairs and Trade is deeply committed to the merit principle, that is, the "best person gets the job."

---

92 "Women in Leadership Strategy: Promoting Equality and Dismantling Barriers," The Australian Government Department of Foreign Affairs and Trade Women in Leadership Strategy, November 2015.

"When you start to unpack merit, you realize that it's not an entirely objective assessment," she says. "But if you have a target then it can coexist more comfortably with a merit system rather than a quota."

According to the plan, targets were set for the representation of women at two levels of leadership to achieve a 40-40-20 gender balance by 2020. The breakdown was to be 40 percent women, 40 percent men, and 20 percent either.[93] These levels were based on evidence from the consultant firm that "workplace culture becomes more gender-inclusive in organizations with more than 40 percent of women in senior leadership positions."

Cooper describes how a quota for the number of women in certain roles is predicated on the hope that "there is a certain number of women who can do the job coming through your doors." That system ran the risk that people may be put into positions that aren't the correct fit, solely to fill a quota. On the other hand, the goal is to have enough women who are applying or presenting themselves for opportunities for which they are qualified. The organization's assessment found that "it wasn't that women were less competent, [but that] they were less *confident.*" Changing the culture was necessary as it directly impacted the confidence factor as well.

At the time of the plan's creation, 25 percent of Cooper's leadership level were women. By the end of 2018, that number had increased to 32 percent, which was "significant" progress toward the target of 35 percent. By November 2019, the

---

93   Ibid.

Ministry hit the 2020 40 percent target a full year ahead of the plan.[94]

The plan also took out another glass ceiling by making all roles flexible throughout the organization. This mandated flexibility for working hours, working from home, and communicating with the manager to make it possible. This, Cooper says, changed the culture of Australia's foreign affairs workforce. She remarks, "It has been significant because it has made a broader range of people feel that they can commit to their career and be able to organize it [so] that they can meet other commitments which are oftentimes family-related."

Another part of the plan was changing the photos displayed in official buildings. It ended up being "very powerful," Cooper described. "When you walk into a building, they often have long rows of framed photos of the men who have led the organization." The implementation group "scoured all the archives for historical photos of women." To make sure there was more gender balance in the photo displays even if women weren't pictured from historical times, they decided that with each historical display there would also be a contemporary display featuring women leaders.

The goal was to remember the history and for women to be able to see themselves reflected in the fabric of the organization. I agree that organizations often overlook this important aspect. I recall walking through prominent hallways of the organizations I have worked for and seeing framed photographs of the organizations' presidents lining the white walls.

---

94 Ibid.

More often than not, over a century of white men stared back at me while I slowly shrunk into a cascading feeling of "Where do I fit in?" The progress Cooper describes reminds me of a broader message I heard in multiple interviews: when it comes to photos, role models, and leadership positions, it helps if you can see yourself in them.

Cooper recounts that before the plan was implemented, all the names of meeting rooms in government buildings had been named after men or flowers. Bemused, she says, "It's really absurd, right?" Through the plan, the group changed all the meeting room names of flowers to Australian women who had made significant contributions to foreign affairs and international relations. Cooper remembers how "powerful" that was, because for every room, whether named after a man or woman, they added small plaques with a bio and a photo of the person. Anyone entering a meeting room could now learn about different men and women leaders, and the small change educated people about famous Australians in the field.

The goal of the plan was to "showcase women and men role models." I can tell you first-hand that in many Washington buildings, whether affiliated with a government, a hotel, or an organization, meeting rooms are often named after men—either leaders or prominent donors of organizations. I've been in rooms named Washington, Jefferson, Lincoln, and Cherry Blossom. Rarely do I come across meeting or conference rooms named after women.

The successor of Peter Varghese was Secretary Frances Adamson. Cooper says, "She was completely on board with the agenda and has taken it to a whole new level." Adamson has "looked very closely at ambassadors overseas," as she is determined to make sure there is a "good representation of women as there are some places that have never had women ambassadors." In the Washington Embassy where we're seated, Cooper points to the table and looks around the room. "There's never been a woman Ambassador here, for example."

While she is committed to the movement of women in leadership and the women's agenda, Cooper underlines the importance of ensuring women are at the table when "hard" issues like national security or economic policy are discussed. Cooper asserts, "There is a place for events where women can discuss gender equity and share their experiences; however, these events alone are not enough to make a difference in women's representation at senior levels." Cooper believes that in diplomacy, you need both genders looking at hard issues just as much as soft issues such as culture and multilateral institutions.

According to Cooper, "Hard issues are often associated with men dominating the table." One of her earliest meetings she attended in Washington was a high-level round table discussion with forty people. They gathered at the Embassy to discuss technology and cybersecurity. She looked at the faces seated at the table. Out of forty, around three were women.

After the meeting, she quipped, "It's so interesting that there aren't more women in Washington who work on these issues."

"What do you mean?" was the response.

"Did you not see the composition of the people around the room?" she asked.

The gender imbalance at the table had not registered. When she officially started her post as Deputy Head of Mission, her first step was making everyone conscious of the need to ensure women's voices were present and heard. When she receives an event guest list dominated by men, she sends it back and asks for gender parity.

Another thing Cooper prominently addresses is gender balance on panels. She was "shocked" to see the imbalance of women representation in meetings focused on national security and foreign policy and overall, in the Washington panel circuit. A few of the men working on the subject matter responded to her by sighing, "There's just not that many women in this space." On the flip side, when she spoke with women who work in national security and foreign policy, they also sighed, "We hear it all the time, and it's just crazy."

Cooper counters this notion by ensuring she has a long list of women experts and for events she hosts, there is always a strong women contingent. Cooper mentions the idea of the "panel pledge," a concept she learned from former Commissioner Elizabeth Broderick.[95] When leaders are asked to be involved or sponsor a panel or conference, they ensure women leaders are represented. When a leader is invited to participate on a panel, for example, they agree to it only if women are also represented. If the organizer doesn't know

---

95   "Commit to the Panel Pledge," Male Champions of Change, updated June 3, 2019.

any women in the field, the leader can provide some options of women experts.

The panel pledge actively promotes and pushes for women to be well represented on panels. It supports three goals in particular:

1. Getting rid of "manels," or all-male panels.

2. Making women more visible, boosting their career trajectory, and providing role models for emerging women leaders.

3. Ensuring women are included in panels that focus on hard and substantive issues in addition to gender related topics.

Cooper asserts, "We can't just talk about gender issues, we have to talk about substantive issues. But we shouldn't [also] pretend gender isn't an issue . . . because it is."

In a private conversation, a colleague of mine mentions that early in her career when she was serving as an intern on Capitol Hill, she sat in a briefing with around 150 people. She slowly looked around the room and realized in the audience, she was one of three women. It's one thing to notice who is on a panel, but we also need to look at who is in the room. The composition of an audience can be just as important as who is leading the discussion.

Each generation makes strides for gender equality. Seasoned colleagues of Cooper's have reminded her that she wasn't the first to contribute to the movement. "Every generation needs to take a step forward," Cooper declares. From our conversation, I learn that proper gender equity and equality also means giving men opportunities to do things that they can't do or get stigmatized for doing. It's a two-way street.

Cooper maintains that in addition to finding ways to bring women together, we need to look at how we change a culture and how people are thinking about it. "I think it's just common sense. We are half of the population. Why wouldn't we be there?"

While Cooper has worked with many "intelligent, powerful, and capable women," she noticed that a primary driver in a career is having the "confidence to speak up, speak out, and back yourself." It echoes back to early in her career, when she was the only woman at the table. "Although I failed to persuade anybody at that time," recounts Cooper, she continues to "make her points." Her ultimate advice is to have confidence and to be good at what you do by being competent, professional, and prepared. Ultimately, you must enjoy your work. "The day you stop enjoying what you do, it's the day to get another job," laughs Cooper.

If you're going to have a strong effective organization, you need diversity. Diversity drives balance.

CHAPTER 16

THE ULTIMATE BALANCE

———

*"The size of your dreams must always
exceed your current capacity to achieve
them. If your dreams do not scare
you, they are not big enough."*

—ELLEN JOHNSON SIRLEAF
FORMER PRESIDENT OF LIBERIA AND FIRST
ELECTED WOMAN HEAD OF STATE IN AFRICA

Driving diversity is a crucial part of the solution for ultimate balance. Another aspect of diplomacy to consider is
the balance of substance and leadership. Foreign policy and
issue experts cannot thrive in a vacuum. Leadership and
management are necessary in team-building. Lone Dencker
Wisborg is a champion for this idea of balancing leadership
and management. She was raised in a home where her Danish parents shared equal power and responsibility to nurture
her and her older brother. "They had the same expectations
of both of us," Wisborg recounts.

Wisborg never felt constrained by barriers, and with this mentality, she rose in the ranks of the Danish Ministry of Foreign Affairs and became Denmark's Ambassador to the U.S. on April 8, 2019.

Wisborg's leadership experience consists of multiple senior level roles, including State Secretary and Chief Operating Officer in the Ministry of Foreign Affairs, Ambassador of Denmark to Spain from 2011 to 2015, Undersecretary for Global Security from 2009 to 2011, and Head of Department for Security Policy from 2007 to 2009. Wisborg held a position as Chief Operating Officer for the Bikuben Foundation from 2006 to 2007. (But wait, there's more.)

Prior to this, Wisborg served as Deputy Head of Mission in Warsaw from 2004 to 2006 and as Private Secretary to the Minister for Foreign Affairs from 2001 to 2003. She also served as Head of Section in the International Department of the Danish Parliament from 1999 to 2000, and First Secretary at the Embassy of Denmark in Estonia and Head of Section in the Ministry of Foreign Affairs. Her resume is bursting at the seams.

Wisborg is tall in stature and has light seafoam blue-green eyes. She wears a gray sweater dress and a white scarf. The deep timbre of her voice exudes focus and confidence.

She speaks directly, yet I find her to be highly approachable and expressive with a great sense of humor. Upon my arrival, Wisborg welcomes me to sit at a circular table in her office. The windows overlook the cascading trees of Dumbarton Oaks. The white rectangular room is modern with sleek finishes of floating wooden shelves. Our conversation bounces off the minimalist walls.

During one of her first leadership appointments in the Security Policy Department, Wisborg led a team that worked closely with the Ministry of Defense. She recalls that when she began, there was a "trench warfare mentality" that was all about winning or losing. If the Foreign Ministry won, the Defense Ministry had to lose. The reverse was also true. According to Wisborg, "It was very much about big egos, winning, and not letting the shield down." That's not her mode of operation. A background in diplomacy had taught Wisborg how to work with different stakeholders. This was Wisborg's first opportunity to put it into practice.

Wisborg gathered her staff and explained how their Ministry had very common interests with the Defense Ministry, as they agreed on 95 percent of the issues. She then asked her team, "If we agree on 95 percent, why are we fighting each other so much? Why are we so focused on winning and losing?" She encouraged the group to put aside their egos and talk about the issues. Since the difficult part was the last 5 percent where they disagreed, Wisborg suggested they "put it on a table and try to see if both groups can find solutions that were mutually beneficial."

Wisborg said, "Let's find solutions that we can both live with. Maybe there's one issue that's very important to them, and not so important to us so we can give them that. And then there are areas where we have a really big interest and they might not care as much."

It was a completely different philosophy. She could see her staff getting a little worried. Their faces portrayed anxious feelings: "She's giving it all away, she's putting it on the table. Maybe the Ministry of Defense will take it all and we will be stripped naked!" However, the method was a great success and the team admitted it later. "In reality, when you put it all on the table, very often you can find good solutions," determined Wisborg.

This is a transparency with which Wisborg operates. Instead of hidden agendas or trying to win so others will lose, Wisborg puts all options on the table.

She affirms that "You can always find solutions that both parties can live with. Then it turns into a win-win situation. People become much more productive and creative when they don't need to watch their backs."

In our conversation, Wisborg is hesitant to discuss differences between male and female mentalities. She says, "Both men and women have overlapping attributes," but cautions that, "men are focused on winning and women are focused on getting things done."

Wisborg finds that women are far less obsessed about who did what and who gets credit as long as the problem is resolved. She explains that if a group chooses not to obsess about "who does what" and what "kind of light falls on you," it's often easier to get results. This is a psychological tool Wisborg has used in many diplomatic negotiations. She says it is best to try to get the person you're negotiating with to come to your desired solution on their own, as it's much better if they own the idea and launch it. If you shed your ego, it's far easier to get results.

For Wisborg, leadership and diplomacy are very much about psychology, understanding the individual stakeholder, and finding out their positions and their mindset. Then you can find ways to move the other party to compromise. Consider what you might offer them without compromising your own needs. Employing psychology in diplomacy is part of the job for Wisborg, whether negotiating with diplomats or motivating her staff.

In foreign ministries and diplomacy in general, people are very competitive. Wisborg jokes, "They enter and they want to be the boss." The pivotal moment of finding balance in leadership was when Wisborg realized that an effective leader can get results through others. She says, "I found that it's not particularly important to do things myself and to claim the fame."

Wisborg loves to see her staff succeed; she says it's far more rewarding to see her staff understand a situation, tackle it, and achieve a result than to take credit.

Wisborg discusses how she began to develop her leadership skills during her posting as Deputy Head of Mission in Warsaw. She arrived, confident in her certain management style of delegating. "I like when people take responsibility if they know better than I do what to do in a particular field. I will give overall direction and coach them, but I expect them to try to fill out their jobs themselves." She realized that the same approach doesn't always fit in different work cultures, especially in an environment where people are used to being told what to do.

Wisborg says she is more familiar with a very flat hierarchy, which she attributes to the Danish way of making independent decisions and challenging authority. However, at the Embassy in Warsaw, it was a different tradition. She quickly learned that for everyone to work well, she needed to meet the people where they were in their working style. It made a big impression on her that when you arrive in a new role and location, you can come with all your ideas and philosophies, but they may not apply to the people or the situation. For people to start moving in the same direction, a leader must pick up their team where they are, then guide them to where they need to be.

Wisborg says that being an Ambassador goes "a little bit against her nature." There are things and issues you cannot delegate as you are the top staff member representing your country. It is a balancing act for her. She must distinguish between the things only she can do and the things her staff and colleagues can achieve. She often reflects on what works and doesn't work to refine her approach. "It's not a one-size-fits-all [approach] because people are different," she claims, "and people are motivated by different management styles."

Early in Wisborg's career—during a European regional meeting of all Danish ambassadors and DCMs—she started to notice the absence of women. At a table of thirty people, she recalls seeing only one other woman. She was also struck by the meeting's agenda—that they only discussed foreign policy issues and mentioned nothing of leadership or the management of the embassies.

In a group of diplomat leaders, most tend to focus on what they find to be the substantive issues of foreign policy. However,

Wisborg believes the other part of the equation is the management and facilitation of that foreign policy. She stresses the importance of learning how to manage a team in order to reach the best achievable outcome—the necessity of balancing the substance of foreign policy with management and leadership. Without good management, teams cannot thrive for maximum effectiveness. As an example, Wisborg says that taking team members "out of their silos" for cross-collaboration allows individuals to join efforts and use creativity.

"It took me a long time to realize that there was a gender issue in diplomacy because I never felt it personally. I didn't find any barriers. I didn't bump into a glass ceiling," Wisborg recalls. It wasn't until 2015 when she joined the Ministry's senior management team and started seeing the actual data showing that women weren't in leading positions. She asked herself, "Why aren't [women] there?" The Danish Foreign Ministry ended up becoming one of the first public institutions to publish the percentages of women joining the field and the number of women in varying leadership roles.

At the time, the Permanent Secretary who led the Ministry in Denmark was also an economist. He became a gender equality champion by looking at the data and leading the charge to do something. They decided they wanted to increase the number of women in positions every year. That decision "drove the development" of gender parity in the Ministry.

Wisborg says that looking at the data was one thing, but tackling the issue directly was another. The senior management team sat around the table for their annual meeting; they discussed the plan to rotate ambassadors, deputy chiefs of missions, and heads of departments. This meeting was also when the group decided who to appoint for their first managerial positions. Wisborg recalls, "looking at the individual posts and matching the applicants."

She continues, "We'd look at a post and find [that] the man was better suited for it. Then we went to another post and found that another man was suited for it." At first Wisborg agreed, as the appointments seem to make sense. As the meeting continued, a pattern emerged, and she realized, "Something is wrong here." While the criteria for posts had been developed over centuries, she saw that the people who determined the criteria had all been men. She found the problem: the person defining the playing field also defines the players. Thus, Wisborg questioned the method: "Who says it has to be defined that way? Maybe we can define it another way."

It may seem obvious, for example, that a man who has been working on Russian policy should be the choice to lead the department focusing on Russia. However, there may be a woman candidate better suited to get more out of her team than the man, or vice versa. The centuries-old criteria did not take this "substance versus leadership" into account.

Wisborg steered the group. "We have to think out of the box because we think we're not biased and are making objective decisions on appointments." The group had been staying inside their predetermined playing field, but staying inside the box hampered the group from reimagining the criteria itself. Merit was, of course, important to the group, but how the group looked at the criteria needed to shift. After

Wisborg spoke up, the group reached a "broad acceptance that something needed to change."

Sitting at the circular table in her modern office, Wisborg looks out the window into the forest of trees, then returns her gaze to me. Her expression steely-eyed, "We have a job to try to redefine the playing field."

* * *

In the culmination of my interviews, I've determined eight central ways of driving gender parity:

1. Have the leadership of the organization promote gender parity

2. Redefine the matrix of merit and how we evaluate leadership potential

3. Incorporate innovative parental and family leave policies, including flexible work hours

4. Use targets instead of quotas to build gender parity in a sustainable, merit-based manner

5. Create spaces that represent the people we are serving

6. Give leadership opportunities to younger members of the team to grow their skills

7. Allow room for mistakes and get rid of the notion of perfection

8. Look actively at who's around the table, noting gender, race, ethnicity, religion, and socioeconomic status

While some cultures are more homogenous than others, "the table" should reflect the society it represents. Yes, the list above is short, and we should consider what criteria to add to continue pushing this work forward. What kind of gender parity system exists in your place of work or organization?

Many generations have focused on the issues of gender equality and diversity. The women I have been privileged to interview give me hope for the future. They are actively influencing the course of history. Through these interviews and research, I have discovered how both genders have championed women leaders. As a collective, global community, we need to continue adding to the list.

So, what's the secret? How do we shape who's around the table?

To effectively transform the system, we must change the system itself.

EPILOGUE

———

"Be a craftsman in speech that thou mayest be strong, for the strength of one is the tongue, and speech is mightier than all fighting."

—PTAHHOTEP

FIRST MINISTER, EGYPTIAN FIFTH DYNASTY,
REIGN OF PHARAOH DJEDKARE ISESI

The air is crisp. Part of me wishes I brought a jacket as I leave the Rayburn House Building on a mid-November evening. In a red cab, I drive past the shining U.S. Capitol Building, the elegant Supreme Court where the chandeliers are still lit, and the historic white stone government buildings that fade into the night sky. We are about a week away from the American Thanksgiving holiday.

Each year, my family gathers around a full table, and before we eat dry turkey, we each share what we are grateful for. As I gear up for the holiday, I begin to ask myself, *What are you grateful for this year?* Thoughts swirl intensely in my head. As my mind begins to calm, I think back to earlier in the evening.

I was returning from supporting a reporter friend of mine who had moderated a small discussion after a film screening. Two thoughts came to mind:

1. I have watched and cheered on this friend as she's risen in the ranks of her reporting career to the goal of focusing on foreign policy. Our lady crew group of friends is proud of her and we continue to toast one another through encouragement and sisterhood—a lesson many interviewees mentioned. Support one another.

2. Though I attended the film screening just to say hello, I ended up staying for the screening and post-screening discussion. (To be fair, the mountain of cheese and warm pastry hors d'oeuvres were hard to pass up.) As the reception moved into the film screening, I found myself completely captivated. *The Cave* followed a Syrian doctor as she and her hospital team tried to save lives amidst constant bombing, supply shortages, and the sinking feeling of their reality in a hollowed-out Syria. Watching this on-screen doctor make life-and-death decisions while having her authority questioned because of her gender was profound and mind-boggling. After leaving the screening and discussion with the director and producer, it all started to click. Diplomacy is the tip of the sword. We use it so we don't have to go to battle and plunge deeper, creating a wound we cannot repair.

I began to think about Representative Bayan Rahman from the Kurdistan Regional Government. When she contemplates why she works in diplomacy, the children of her people come to mind. As I watched the film this evening, it was the children in the hospital who stood out. In multiple conversations with ambassadors, deputy chiefs of mission, and diplomats, they mentioned that women often think of the children.

When fostering negotiations and peace agreements, who will think about the next generation? Who will fight for the ultimate goal of peace and stability? Relationships between countries will fail and embassies and consulates will close, signaling a downhill spiral in diplomacy. Sanctions might be drafted. Swords might be drawn. More importantly, the people of a country may suffer. And then, there are the children—the ones who have no voice or means of fighting for themselves. They do not have the option of diplomacy. It is too late.

The necessity of diplomacy is apparent. It's as tangible as the falling leaves of this season. I love Autumn. When the leaves change colors to hues of red, orange, and yellow, my heart expands and a smile spreads on my face. Diplomacy reminds me of the leaves. Relationship building has different hues and can change colors. But once relationships fall, we will irreparably crush their existence if we aren't careful. Both women and men are needed to secure these relationships in every season.

I think about invading forces and the women holding steady, like Ambassador Barbara Bodine in occupied Kuwait and Aggie Kuperman in Tehran. My mind traces back to diplomatic peacekeeping and free elections in Afghanistan, covered by Croatian Deputy Chief of Mission Lara Romano.

For anyone that will listen, I share the wisdom of Swedish Ambassador Karin Olofsdotter and her government's promotion of feminist foreign policy and a paternal leave system to address workplace inequality. And The Diplomat representing the African Muslim majority country reminds us that change is gradual, but we must keep pushing. As Ambassador Melanne Verveer asked, what will you do with your convening power?

I hear the voice of Finnish Ambassador Kirsti Kauppi echo that all positions can make a difference, not just the top. We learned from Hungarian Ambassador Reka Szemerkényi that there is no need to sacrifice your career or family—do both and you will be stronger at the table. Danish Ambassador Long Dencker Wisborg urges us that the building of a team is just as important as who is leading it. Afghan Ambassador Roya Rahmani points out that everything is personal, and quitting is not an option.

Changing a system is possible with vision, according to Australian Ambassador Katrina Cooper. Ambassador Bergdís Ellertsdóttir of Iceland emphasized the importance of treating everyone with respect. We must believe in the power of resilience like Mexican Ambassador Martha Bárcena, and remember how Macedonian Ambassador Ljubica Z. Acevska encouraged us to believe in our work regardless of obstacles. We must empower one another, as nothing can be accomplished alone, according to Ambassador Vlora Çitaku of Kosovo.

May we continue to build coalitions in honor of Lauren Protentis and choose battles worth fighting for like Namibian

Ambassador Monica Nashandi. Deputy Chief of Mission from Singapore Sheryl Shum showed that both confidence and competence are intertwined. As each of us enters a room, I hope we let our music play just as the Honorable Mary Beth Long has done, and let us heed Austrian Ambassador Eva Nowotny who instructed us to use our intellectual curiosity and openness to engage because history is shaped by humans. Hear the questions of U.S. Army Major General Linda Singh ring through your head, "What have you tried? What are you willing to risk? Who are your allies?"

Let the wisdom of Sally Painter seep in, take a risk and remember everything is a job interview. Embrace the generation-length long game like Laure Pallez and take the time to see and feel the culture and community everywhere you go like U.S. Ambassador Lisa Guillermin Gable. Know your goals and go for them as advised by Albanian Ambassador Floreta Faber. Listen to Saint Kitts and Nevis Ambassador Thelma Phillip-Browne and enhance your slot in the tapestry of the universe. When you do reach the pinnacle, embrace Austrian Ambassador Ursula Plassnik's thought that you might feel lonely as a leader but remember that it's part of the journey. Finally, remember UNESCO Director-General Irina Bokova's words that the ability to listen is the basis to ultimately be heard.

* * *

In honor of giving thanks, I offer these words:

Let us not wage war.
Let us use our voices with rigor and thunder.
Let us embody confidence and kindness in an
equal manner.
Let us find ways to build allies and coalitions for a more
peaceful world.
Let diplomacy reign for a free and just society that our
children can be proud of.

ACKNOWLEDGEMENTS

———

Writing this book afforded me the unique opportunity to speak with women from varying fields of diplomacy. Each conversation gave me new insights and made this project a reality. Thank you to all of these leaders for sharing your precious time and stories.

Ambassador Ljubica Z. Acevska
The Republic of North Macedonia

Ambassador Martha Bárcena
The United Mexican States

Ambassador Barbara K. Bodine
The United States of America

Former Director General of UNESCO Irina Bokova
The Republic of Bulgaria

Ambassador Vlora Çitaku
The Republic of Kosovo

Ambassador Katrina Cooper
The Commonwealth of Australia

Ajla Delkic
President of the Advisory Council for Bosnia and
Herzegovina

Corina DuBois
The United States of America

Ambassador Bergdís Ellertsdóttir
Iceland

Ambassador Floreta Faber
The Republic of Albania

Nadia Farra
The United States of America

Kim Kahnhauser Freeman
Executive Director of the Women's Foreign Policy Group

Ambassador Lisa Guillermin Gable
The United States of America

Ambassador Swanee Hunt
The United States of America

Ambassador Kirsti Kauppi
The Republic of Finland

Aggie Kuperman
The United States of America

The Honorable Mary Beth Long
The United States of America

Ambassador Monica Nashandi
The Republic of Namibia

Ambassador Eva Nowotny
The Republic of Austria

Ambassador Karin Olofsdotter
The Kingdom of Sweden

Sally Painter
The United States of America

Laure Pallez
The French Republic

Ambassador Thelma Phillip-Browne
Saint Kitts and Nevis

Ambassador and Former Foreign Minister Ursula Plassnik
The Republic of Austria

Lauren Protentis
The United States of America

Representative Bayan Sami Abdul Rahman
The Kurdistan Regional Government

Ambassador Roya Rahmani
The Islamic Republic of Afghanistan

Deputy Chief of Mission Lara Romano
The Republic of Croatia

Deputy Chief of Mission Sheryl Shum
The Republic of Singapore

U.S. Army Major General Linda Singh
The United States of America

Ambassador Reka Szemerkényi
Hungary

Ambassador Melanne Verveer
The United States of America

Ambassador Lone Dencker Wisborg
The Kingdom of Denmark

WITH GRATITUDE

———

To my family, friends, and colleagues who made this book possible. Whether it was introducing me to your personal connections, setting up interviews, editing chapters, providing tea or much needed chocolate, or simply being a part of the journey—thank you.

A special note to my parents, Sarah and Stan. Both of you have taught me countless lessons such as integrity and kindness. My life and this book are possible because of you.

To Lisa Bennett who led our Georgetown University graduate cohort around the world and introduced me to the Creator Institute. To Eric Koester, Founder of the Creator Institute, who guided this magnificent book experience. To the team at New Degree Press: Karina Agbisit who pushed me to go deeper into the stories, Brian Bies who kept those deadlines rocking no matter what, Elina Oliferovskiy who stepped in giving support and direction, and Leila Summers who read each sentence with precision, respect, and love.

To you, my dear reader, thank you. This book has been a journey and you are now a part of it. I hope you share these lessons as you take your seat at the table.

Adam Bernstein

Adam Lurie

Adam Munitz

Alan Ronkin

Alberta and Jim Muhlbach

Alex Bronzo

Alex Ebsary

Alexa Mata Galindo

Alexandra Moses

Alexandria Keenan

Alida and Steve Lyman

Alissa Platz

Alyssa Bogdanow Arens

Amanda Brown

Amanda Fine

Amy Harbison

Andrea Davis-Hill

Andrew Lyman

Ann Salo

Anna Gawel

Anna Levin

Anne-Charlotte Merrell Wetterwik

Anuradhi Deenamulla

Ari Jacobson

Ariel Bashi

Ásdís Hreinsdóttir

Ashley Mays

Audrey Sandels

Aundrea Paulett

Belle Yoeli

Benjamin Hersch

Bonnie Butler

Brittany Silva

Cecilia Hornum Skogstad

Chana and Michoel Refson

Chelsea Loucks

Christine and David Baker

Christine Fishwick

Colin Shalo

Colleen Reilly

Courtney Campbell

Dani Addison

Daniela Greene

Danielle Langley

Danielle Tobin Mitz

Danny Woods

David Avioli

David Callaghan

David Harris Brown

David Siegman

Dina Siegel Vann

Dr. Stanley Sloan

Eli Ibrahimzade

Elizabeth Jane Via

Ellen Finberg

Emily and Hayden Markette
Eric Sapoznik
Erica and Javier Otero Grau
Erika Wohl
Esma and Jason Isaacson
Ethan Sorcher
Eva Schöfer
Evan Hoffman
Gabrielle Kohlmeier
Gabrielle Leon Spatt
Gavi Geller
Gene Germanovich
Geoffrey Melada
Georgia Rae Hart
Giulia Spaggiari
Gloria Jacobson
Harry Quiett
Helen Arnoldi
Hilary Levine
Ilana Lasday
Ilana Ron Levey
Irene and Mark Rackin
Isaac H. Goldbloom
Jan Hart
Jason Langsner
Jay Lurie
Jeff Kalwerisky
Jen Berman
Jennifer Kessler
Jeremiah Baronberg
Jesse Langley
Jessica Heckerling

Jessica Pantages
Jo and Harmon E. Heed IV
Joanie Taylor
Jodie Schewitz
John O'Neill
John Heneghan
Jonathan Schweitzer
Joseph Simons
Judy Novenstein
Julia Crantz
Julie Willis
Kara Cochran
Karla Bonne
Kayla Gubov
Kelly Healy
Kim DeLapp
Kyle Tortorelli
Laura Kelly
Laura Milstein
Lauren Coleman
Lauren Light
Lawrence Ellison
Leigh Morris Sloane
Liat Dolengiewicz
Lidiya Grankina
Linda Rosenzweig
Lis Kabashi
Liz Brailsford
Louise Spiro
Mamica Toska
Marci Harris-Blumenthal
Maria Ploberg

Mary Merrick
Maryse and Stephen Horblitt
Masha Lora
Matthew Avioli
Matthew Memberg
Melinda K. Gleason
Melissa Urofsky
Metodija Koloski
Micha Kerbel
Michael Leichtman
Michelle and Colin Glover
Mikhail Fogelson
Monica Azhdam
Nina Bruntse Severin
Nina Sundell
Pia Valdivia
Rachel Craig
Randy Tritell
Rebecca Avigad
Rebecca Birch
Rebecca LaBanca
Reggie Galloway
Rev. Leonard L. Hamlin Sr.
Rev. Stacey C. Wilson
Rev. William Lamar, IV
Ricky Clark
Rina Rebibo
Robin Tolochko
Rory Doehring
Rosemary Morris-Castico

Ryan Goldberg
Ryan Pearl
Ryan Shuman
Sam Yolen
Samuel Fischgrund
Santa Molina-Marshall
Sarah Sloan
Seth Kaufman
Shane and Michael Ross
Shari Carson
Sharon Wilkes
Sharon Wilkes Kinberg
Shayna Cherry
Sherry Kaylor
Shiran Zerach
Shereen Hall
Simeon M. Kriesberg
Simone Wilker
Sophie Benson
Stefanie Haroz
Stephen Goss
Susan Renas-Lips
Sylvia Hagenguth
Tarja Aarnio
Thorsten Eisingerich
Tom Snyder
Tyler Rosebush
Una S. Jóhannsdóttir
Zachary Axelrod
Z.B.

APPENDIX

PROLOGUE

- Bindi, Federiga and Mimosa Giamanco. "Missing in Action: The Absence of Women Scholars on Foreign Policy Panels." Georgetown Journal of International Affairs, March 26, 2019. http://www.georgetownjournalofinternationalaffairs.org/online-edition/2019/3/26/missing-in-action-the-absence-of-women-scholars-on-foreign-policy-panels.

- Comparably. "Study: Comparing Compensation & Culture of Millennials & Gen Z." Accessed September 8, 2019. http://www.comparably.com/blog/old-millennials-young-millennials-and-gen-z-comparing-compensation-and-culture.

- Council on Foreign Relations. "Women's Participation in Peace Processes." Updated January 30, 2019. http://www.cfr.org/interactive/womens-participation-in-peace-processes.

- Strano, Andrea. "Foreign Service Women Today: The Palmer Case and Beyond." The Foreign Service Journal, March 2016.

http://www.afsa.org/foreign-service-women-today-palmer-case-and-beyond.

- Tsalikis, Catherine. "The Making of a Gender-Balanced Foreign Service: Stories from the Women Driving Canada's Diplomatic Corps Toward Equality." OpenCanada, April 3, 2018. http://www.opencanada.org/features/making-gender-balanced-foreign-service.

- Weintraub, Leon. "Five Myths About the Foreign Service." The Washington Post, July 20, 2017. http://www.washingtonpost.com/outlook/five-myths/five-myths-about-the-foreign-service/2017/07/20/8aac2a4e-67f5-11e7-8eb5-cbccc2e7bfbf_story.html.

- Zillman, Claire. "The Fortune 500 Has More Female CEOs Than Ever Before." Fortune, May 16, 2019. http://fortune.com/2019/05/16/fortune-500-female-ceos.

CHAPTER 1

- Livemint. "Wing Commander Anjali Singh Becomes India's First Female Military Diplomat." Updated September 17, 2019. http://www.livemint.com/news/india/wing-commander-anjali-singh-becomes-india-s-first-military-diplomat-1568647307429.html.

- Strano, Andrea. "Foreign Service Women Today: The Palmer Case and Beyond." The Foreign Service Journal, March 2016. http://www.afsa.org/foreign-service-women-today-palmer-case-and-beyond.

- Tsalikis, Catherine. "The Making of a Gender-Balanced Foreign Service: Stories from the Women Driving Canada's Diplomatic Corps Toward Equality." OpenCanada, April 3, 2018. http://www.opencanada.org/features/making-gender-balanced-foreign-service.

- Towns, Ann and Birgitta Niklasson. "Gender, International Status, and Ambassador Appointments." Foreign Policy Analysis 13, No. 3 (2016): 521-540. http://doi.org/10.1093/fpa/orw039 (https://doi.org/10.1093/fpa/orw039).

CHAPTER 2

- Bindi, Federiga and Mimosa Giamanco. "Missing in Action: The Absence of Women Scholars on Foreign Policy Panels." Georgetown Journal of International Affairs, March 26, 2019. http://www.georgetownjournalofinternationalaffairs.org/online-edition/2019/3/26/missing-in-action-the-absence-of-women-scholars-on-foreign-policy-panels.

- Central Intelligence Agency. "CIA Makes Progress on Women in Leadership." July 11, 2018. http://www.cia.gov/news-information/featured-story-archive/2018-featured-story-archive/cia-makes-progress-on-women-in-leadership.html.

- Office of the Historian, Foreign Service Institute. United States Department of State. "Women in the Foreign Service." Accessed September 17, 2019. http://history.state.gov/about/faq/women-in-the-foreign-service.

- Sanger E., David and Maggie Haberman. "A Letter From G.O.P. National Security Officials Opposing Donald Trump."

The New York Times, August 8, 2016. http://www.nytimes.com/interactive/2016/08/08/us/politics/national-security-letter-trump.html.

- The Library of Congress, American Memory. "Women Diplomats." Accessed September 17, 2019. http://memory.loc.gov/ammem/awhhtml/awmss5/women_diplo.html.

CHAPTER 3

- African Union. "Silencing the Guns by 2020." Accessed January 15, 2020. http://au.int/en/flagships/silencing-guns-2020.

- Gysman, Nomkhitha. "Zebra Listing: A Way Forward for Women." City Press, May 7, 2018. http://city-press.news24.com/Voices/zebra-listing-a-way-forward-for-women-20180504.

- Simasiku, Obrien."Namibia Ahead of US in Gender Parity, Admits Diplomat." New Era Live, March 25, 2019. http://newer-alive.na/posts/namibia-ahead-of-us-in-gender-parity-admits-diplomat.

- U.S. Embassy Windhoek. "Namibia Becomes First African Country Eligible to Export Beef to the United States." July 13, 2016. http://na.usembassy.gov/namibia-becomes-first-african-country-eligible-export-beef-united-states.

- Witschge, Loes. "African Continental Free Trade Area: What You Need To Know." Al-Jazeera, March 20, 2018. http://www.aljazeera.com/news/2018/03/african-continental-free-trade-area-afcfta-180317191954318.html.

CHAPTER 4

- Asher, Saira. "Barack Obama: Women Are Better Leaders than Men." BBC News, December 16, 2019. https://www.bbc.com/news/world-asia-50805822.

- Barbarani, Sofia. "Meet the Kurdish Female Politician Fighting the Islamic State." The Telegraph. February 20, 2015. https://www.telegraph.co.uk/women/womens-politics/11393823/Islamic-State-Meet-the-Kurdish-female-politician-fighting-it.html.

- Krause, Jana, Werner Krause, and Piia Bränfors. "Women's Participation in Peace Negotiations and the Durability of Peace." International Interactions 44, no. 6 (2018): 985-1016. August 10, 2018. http://doi.org/10.1080/03050629.2018.1492386.

- Towns, Ann and Karin Aggestam. "The Gender Turn in Diplomacy: A New Research Agenda." International Feminist Journal of Politics 21, No.1 (2018): 9-28. http://doi.org/10.1080/14616742.2018.1483206 (https://doi.org/10.1080/14616742.2018.1483206)

- UN Security Council. "Report of the Secretary-General on Women, Peace, and Security." October 9, 2019. S/2019/800, 2019: 6. http://undocs.org/en/S/2019/800 (https://undocs.org/en/S/2019/800).

- UN Security Council. "Report of the Secretary-General on Women, Peace, and Security." October 9, 2019. S/2019/800, 2019: 13. http://undocs.org/en/S/2019/800 (https://undocs.org/en/S/2019/800).

- "Who Are the Kurds?" BBC News, October 15, 2019. http://www.bbc.com/news/world-middle-east-29702440.

- "World Military Expenditure Grows to $1.8 Trillion in 2018." Stockhold International Peace Research Institute, April 29, 2019. http://www.sipri.org/media/press-release/2019/world-military-expenditure-grows-18-trillion-2018.

CHAPTER 5

- Greene, David. "Albright: U.N. Needs To Show Its Relevance On Syrian Issue." Morning Edition. NPR, September 26, 2013. https://www.npr.org/2013/09/26/226375391/albright-u-n-needs-to-show-its-relevance-on-syrian-issue.

- Kandić, Nataša, Patrick Ball PhD, and Michael Spagat. "Kosovo Memory Book Database." National Library "Pjetër Bogdani," Prishtina, February 4, 2015. http://www.kosovomemorybook.org/wp-content/uploads/2015/02/Expert_Evaluation_of_Kosovo_Memory_Book_Database_Prishtina_04_02_2015.pdf

- Krieger, Heike. "The Kosovo Conflict and International Law: An Analytical Documentation 1974-1999." Cambridge University Press (2001): 90, accessed January 18, 2020. http://books.google.com/books?id=-OhPTJn8ZWoC&pg=PA90&d-q=kosovo+1.2+million+albanians+displaced&hl=en#v=onep-age&q=kosovo%201.2%20million%20albanians%20&f=false.

- The United Nations Institute for Disarmament Research (UNIDIR). "Gender & Disarmament Resource Pack for Multilateral Practitioners." January 2019. http://www.unidir.org/files/publications/pdfs/gender-disarmament-resource-pack-en-735.pdf.

CHAPTER 6

- Allam, Hannah. "Women In National Security Push To Move Beyond 'The First' And 'The Only.'" NPR, July 6, 2019. http://www.npr.org/2019/07/06/738988815/women-in-national-security-push-to-move-beyond-the-first-and-the-only?utm_campaign=npr&utm_term=nprnews&utm_medium=social&utm_source=twitter.com.

- Centers for Disease Control and Prevention. "About the CDC-Kaiser ACE Study." Updated April 2, 2019. http://www.cdc.gov/violenceprevention/childabuseandneglect/acestudy/about.html.

- Kidder, Katherine, Amy Schafer, Phillip Carter, and Andrew Swick. "From College to Cabinet: Women in National Security." Center for a New American Security, February 2017. http://s3.amazonaws.com/files.cnas.org/documents/CNAS-Report-WomeninNatSec-Final.pdf?mtime=20170403112013.

- Maryland Global Initiative for Cybersecurity. "Major General Linda L. Singh." University of Maryland. Accessed December 2019. http://magic.umd.edu/aboutsummitspeakers/mg-singh.html.

- Roy, Eleanor Ainge. "'Charismatic' New Zealand PM Jacinda Ardern named Pacific person of the year." The Guardian, January 6, 2020. http://www.theguardian.com/world/2020/jan/07/charismatic-new-zealand-pm-jacinda-ardern-named-pacific-person-of-the-year.

- The Center for Strategic and International Studies. "Global Perceptions of the U.S." CSPAN video, 1:19:30. January 16,

2018. http://www.c-span.org/video/?439823-1/foreign-ambas-sadors-discuss-global-perceptions-us.

- The Her Power Index. "How the U.S. Government Is Failing Women in Foreign Policy." Foreign Policy, October 15, 2019. http://foreignpolicy.com/2019/10/15/us-government-fail-ing-women-foreign-policy-her-power-index.

- Wenger, Yvonne Wenger. "Damage to Businesses from Balti-more Rioting Estimated at About $9 Million." The Washing-ton Post, May 13, 2015. http://www.washingtonpost.com/local/damage-to-businesses-from-baltimore-rioting-estimated-at-9-million/2015/05/13/5848c3fe-f9a8-11e4-a13c-193b1241d51a_story.html.

CHAPTER 7
- UN Women. "Women Refugees and Migrants." Accessed Jan-uary 19, 2020. http://www.unwomen.org/en/news/in-focus/women-refugees-and-migrants#notes.

CHAPTER 8
- Avonius, Leena, Meeri-Maria Jaarva, Ulrike Schmidt, and Talia Wohl. "Inclusion of Women and Effective Peace Pro-cesses: A Toolkit," Organization for Security and Co-operation in Europe (OSCE). Accessed January 12, 2020. http://www.osce.org/secretariat/440735?download=true.

- Clinton Global Initiative. "Empowering Girls & Women." Accessed January 25, 2020. http://www.un.org/en/ecosoc/phl-ntrpy/notes/clinton.pdf.

- Council on Foreign Relations. "Women's Participation in Peace Processes." Updated January 30, 2019. http://www.cfr.org/interactive/womens-participation-in-peace-processes.

- Wharton School of the University of Pennsylvania. "Does Gender Diversity on Boards Really Boost Company Performance?" May 18, 2017. http://knowledge.wharton.upenn.edu/article/will-gender-diversity-boards-really-boost-company-performance.

CHAPTER 9

- Council on Foreign Relations. "Women's Participation in Peace Processes." Updated January 30, 2019. http://www.cfr.org/interactive/womens-participation-in-peace-processes.

- Chakrabarti, Oisika and Sharon Grobeisen, "Media advisory: UN Women Highlights the Voices of Women Building Sustainable Peace and Mobilizing for Justice and Equality." UN Women, October 23, 2017. http://www.unwomen.org/en/news/stories/2017/10/media-advisory-un-women-at-open-debate-on-security-council-resolution-1325.

- Chicago PBS. "The Devil in the White City," WTTW News. Accessed July 27, 2019. http://interactive.wttw.com/timemachine/devil-white-city.

- Grant Thornton International. "Women in Business: Building a Blueprint for Action." March 2019. http://www.grantthornton.global/globalassets/global-insights---do-not-edit/2019/women-in-business/gtil-wib-report_grant-thornton-spreads-lowres.pdf.

- Krause, Jana, Werner Krause, and Piia Bränfors. "Women's Participation in Peace Negotiations and the Durability of Peace." International Interactions 44, no. 6 (2018): 985-1016. August 10, 2018. http://doi.org/10.1080/03050629.2018.1492386.

- Picker, Les. "Where Are ISIS's Foreign Fighters Coming From?" The NBER Digest. The National Bureau of Economic Research, June 2016. http://www.nber.org/digest/jun16/w22190.html.

- Rowan, Mattisan. "ISIS After the Caliphate." The Wilson Center. Updated January 8, 2018. http://www.wilsoncenter.org/article/isis-after-the-caliphate-0.

- Sly, Liz. "Islamic State May Still Have 30,000 Fighters in Iraq and Syria, Even After Setbacks." The Washington Post, August 14, 2018. http://www.washingtonpost.com/world/islamic-state-may-still-have-30000-fighters-in-iraq-and-syria-even-after-setbacks/2018/08/14/f929cbe2-9fd6-11e8-a3dd-2a1991f075d5_story.html.

- Tyson, Laura D'Andrea. "Gender Parity Can Boost Economic Growth. Here's How." World Economic Forum, March 8, 2019. http://www.weforum.org/agenda/2019/03/how-to-fix-gender-pay-gap-laura-tyson.

- UN Security Council. "Report of the Secretary-General on Women, Peace, and Security." October 9, 2019. S/2019/800, 2019: 6. http://undocs.org/en/S/2019/800 (https://undocs.org/en/S/2019/800).

CHAPTER 10

- Abend, Lisa. "Finland's Sanna Marin, the World's Youngest Female Head of Government, Wants Equality, Not Celebrity." *Time*. Accessed February 2, 2020. http://time.com/collection/davos-2020/5764097/sanna-marin-finland-equality.

- Anderson, Rania H. "Challenging Our Gendered Idea of Mentorship." Harvard Business Review, January 6, 2020. http://hbr.org/2020/01/challenging-our-gendered-idea-of-mentorship.

- Catalyst. "Women in Management: Quick Take." August 7, 2019. http://www.catalyst.org/research/women-in-management.

- Niethammer, Carmen. "Finland's New Government Is Young And Led By Women—Here's What The Country Does To Promote Diversity." Forbes, December 12, 2019. http://www.forbes.com/sites/carmenniethammer/2019/12/12/finlands-new-government-is-young-and-led-by-women-heres-what-the-country-does-to-promote-diversity/#69ca1e4635aa.

CHAPTER 11

- Bewig, Matt Bewig. "Ambassador of Sweden to the United States: Who Is Karin Olofsdotter?" AllGov, December 3, 2017. http://www.allgov.com/news/top-stories/ambassador-of-sweden-to-the-united-states-who-is-karin-olofsdotter-171203?news=860379.

CHAPTER 12

- Abass, Jamila. "Women Grow 70% of Africa's Food. But Have Few Rights Over the Land They Tend." World Economic Forum, March 21, 2018. http://www.weforum.org/agenda/2018/03/women-farmers-food-production-land-rights.

- Avonius, Leena, Meeri-Maria Jaarva, Ulrike Schmidt, and Talia Wohl. "Inclusion of Women and Effective Peace Processes: A Toolkit," Organization for Security and Co-operation in Europe (OSCE). Accessed January 12, 2020. http://www.osce.org/secretariat/440735?download=true.

- Dalaqua, Renata Hessmann, Kjølv Egeland, and Torbjørn Graff Hugo, "Still Behind the Curve: Gender Balance in Arms Control, Non-Proliferation and Disarmament Diplomacy." The United Nations Institute for Disarmament Research (UNIDIR), 2019. http://www.unidir.org/files/publications/pdfs/still-behind-the-curve-en-770.pdf.

- Gíslason, Ingólfur V. "Parental Leave in Iceland Gives Dad a Strong Position." Nordic Labour Journal, April 12, 2019. http://www.nordiclabourjournal.org/i-fokus/in-focus-2019/future-of-work-iceland/article.2019-04-11.9299118347.

- Gunn, Dwyer. "How Should Parental Leave Be Structured? Ask Iceland." Slate, April 3, 2013. http://slate.com/human-interest/2013/04/paternity-leave-in-iceland-helps-mom-succeed-at-work-and-dad-succeed-at-home.html.

- Hafstað, Vala. "More than 50,000 Immigrants in Iceland." Iceland Monitor, December 2, 2019. http://icelandmonitor.mbl.is/

news/news/2019/12/02/more_than_50_000_immigrants_in_
iceland.

- Jakobsdóttir, Katrín. "How to Build a Paradise for Women. A
  Lesson from Iceland." World Economic Forum, November 23,
  2018. http://www.weforum.org/agenda/2018/11/iceland-para-
  dise-for-women-katr%C3%ADn-jakobsdottir.

- "Population of Iceland Has Now Topped 350,000: Immigrants Make Up 11.3% of Population." Iceland Magazine,
  May 2, 2018. http://icelandmag.is/article/population-ice-
  land-has-now-topped-350000-immigrants-make-113-popula-
  tion.

- The Center for Gender Equality Iceland. "Gender Equality in
  Iceland: Information on Gender Issues in Iceland." February
  2012. http://www.althingi.is/pdf/wip/Gender_Equality_in_Ice-
  land_2012.pdf.

CHAPTER 13

- Avonius, Leena, Meeri-Maria Jaarva, Ulrike Schmidt, and
  Talia Wohl. "Inclusion of Women and Effective Peace Processes: A Toolkit," Organization for Security and Co-operation
  in Europe (OSCE). Accessed January 12, 2020. http://www.osce.
  org/secretariat/440735?download=true.

- Beard, Alison. "Women Respond Better Than Men to
  Competitive Pressure." Harvard Business Review, November-December 2017. http://hbr.org/2017/11/women-respond-bet-
  ter-than-men-to-competitive-pressure.

- Kelly, Michael. "The Rape and Rescue of Kuwaiti City: Torture Victims and Tense Victors." The New Republic, March 24, 1991. http://newrepublic.com/article/76724/rape-rescue-kuwait-iraq-saddam-hussein.

- "Kuwait: Rape of a Nation." Newsweek, March 10, 1991. http://www.newsweek.com/kuwait-rape-nation-201584.

- Luxner, Larry. "Afghanistan's First Female Ambassador to U.S. Insists Peace Is Still Possible." The Washington Diplomat, December 3, 2019. http://washdiplomat.com/index.php?option=com_content&view=article&id=20991&Itemid=413.

- Taylor, Alan. "The Soviet War in Afghanistan, 1979 - 1989." The Atlantic, August 4, 2014. http://www.theatlantic.com/photo/2014/08/the-soviet-war-in-afghanistan-1979-1989/100786.

- The United Nations Institute for Disarmament Research (UNIDIR). "Gender & Disarmament Resource Pack for Multilateral Practitioners." January 2019. http://www.unidir.org/files/publications/pdfs/gender-disarmament-resource-pack-en-735.pdf.

CHAPTER 14

- Bävman, Johan. "Swedish Dads." Accessed January 16, 2020. http://www.johanbavman.se/swedish-dads.

- Dalaqua, Renata Hessmann, Kjølv Egeland, and Torbjørn Graff Hugo, "Still Behind the Curve: Gender Balance in Arms Control, Non-Proliferation and Disarmament Diplomacy." The

United Nations Institute for Disarmament Research (UNIDIR), 2019. http://www.unidir.org/files/publications/pdfs/still-be-hind-the-curve-en-770.pdf.

- Duncan, Gillian. "Women are Making Strides in Diplomacy, But Progress is Painfully Slow." The National, November 19, 2018. http://www.thenational.ae/uae/women-are-making-strides-in-diplomacy-but-progress-is-painfully-slow-1.793202.

- World Bank Group. "Women, Business and the Law 2016: Getting to Equal." Accessed January 20, 2020. http://pubdocs. worldbank.org/en/458191519943376087/4pager-WBL2017-Child-Care.pdf.

CHAPTER 15

- Male Champions of Change. "Commit to the Panel Pledge." Updated June 3, 2019. http://malechampionsofchange.com/commit-to-the-panel-pledge.

- The Australian Government Department of Foreign Affairs and Trade Women in Leadership Strategy. "Women in Leadership Strategy: Promoting Equality and Dismantling Barriers." November 2015. http://dfat.gov.au/about-us/publications/Documents/women-in-leadership-strategy.pdf.